BORN TO PROSPER

KEYS TO UNLOCKING YOUR POTENTIAL

VC Isaacs

Publishing
THR3E 3RED

BORN TO PROSPER

VC ISAACS

THR3E 3RED PUBLISHER

ISBN 978-0-9873619-4-3

BOOK ORDERS: www.victorisaacs.com Email: info@victorisaacs.com

First Publication: 2019

MANUSCRIPT LAYOUT AND EDIT: Adele Visser
Cell: +27(0)82-635-2742 (South Africa)
e-mail: visser969@gmail.com

SPECIAL THANKS

In life, for better or for worse we are what and who we are because of the people in our lives. I want to thank the people in my life. People who speak into my life and challenge me to be better in my walk with God, family and entrepreneurship.

I would also like to thank and dedicate this book to people who are passionate about challenging mediocrity and poverty mindsets. Small thinking has never benefited anyone.

May you discover and unlock the greatness within you as you read this book. I pray that increase, success and prosperity be your portion.

My gratitude would be incomplete without acknowledging the Father, Son and Holy Spirit for their unceasing love and fellowship.

Publishing
THR3E 3RED

ENDORSEMENT

"It's very much a book that's hard to put down. From start to finish *Born to Prosper* is grounded so solidly in the Word of God and is impeccably structured - from His masterplan for humankind via solid logic to personal coaching for success.

All this deep wisdom is then leavened with some great financial facts and some revealing personal sharing of Victor's own journey. It's a Winner!

~ Roger Holden
Franchisee, The Coffee Club Burpengary Trustee
Kingdom Resource Network

FOREWORD

In all my friendships with church Pastors, never have I found someone with such a depth of understanding regarding prosperity and wealth creation as VC Isaacs. Over the past 10 years I have witnessed first-hand how VC has studied and personally put into practice the principles of prosperity. This has been even more fascinating to me knowing something of his early life in Africa. I have listened to his stories of early ventures as a young boy growing up poor, but motivated to avoid living the rest of his life as a victim of poverty. Now established in a new country and having proven the Biblical basis of these principles himself, he is passionate about sharing from his personal experiences.

This book is for those of us who are willing to put aside our fears that prosperity will lead us into a less spiritual life. It is the spiritual basis of prosperity which is so generally ignored and misunderstood. VC takes us as his readers on a journey to discover that prosperity is more than money. However, one can hardly be prosperous without accumulating money as well.

He takes us on a journey beginning with the early patriarchs. Then he explains how they created wealth based on the promises God gave them. He also explains the inheritances they left to succeeding generations. It's important that we know why God intended us to create something that will help our successors reach even greater heights.

With this solid foundation of knowledge, we learn how to go about creating and communicating our own dream. Then what it takes to bring that dream into being. We learn that there are important keys to establishing intergenerational wealth. And we learn how to rewrite our story and live our dream.

We need to know that God expects a return on his investment in each one of us. We are here for a cause greater than ourselves. The two most important days in each person's life are the day you were born, and the day you realized why you were born and discovered your purpose. Jesus was the only person in all human history who was born to be poor and to die. We were each born to live, excel and prosper. Jesus came that we may have more life, abundant life. God gave me a challenging revelation many years ago. He showed me that the most selfish people are those whose only goal is to work so they achieve just enough to enable their families to live a comfortable life.

I realized that we each have a duty to do the best we can. The best of which we are capable, without limiting ourselves to our own needs and wants. To look for ways to help others from the overflowing abundance such an attitude will produce in us.

Poverty and lack do not glorify God. Being prosperous, like the good Samaritan, better enables us to not just pray for others but to be a practical blessing to the needy around us! Imagine how you will feel being able to donate a Million Dollars to meet the need that's closest to your heart! Because, money is just energy. You must use it to power the things you believe in!

Steve Wanmer
Director
ActionCOACH Business Coaching

Keys To Unlocking Your Potential

VC ISAACS

CONTENTS

INTRODUCTION

I felt compelled to write this book about success, prosperity and finances in the same way I feel to write about marriage.

Marriage, finances, success and prosperity are among the top issues people often ask me to pray with them for a breakthrough. The more I listen, the more apparent it has become to me that these challenges are not just a matter of spiritual breakthrough but also practical knowledge and understanding.

Many times, I conclude these prayer or counselling sessions with a sense of wonder. If someone had taken time to explain some simple dynamics of success, prosperity, finances or marriage, it would have made a huge difference in people's lives.

So, this is me taking time to share with you some insights which I believe will bring you to a place of breakthrough to succeed and prosper in your life.

Not that I consider myself a Guru. But I have been broke many times so I can only share from my experiences and some principles which have benefited me immensely.

Don't read this book as financial advice because it's not, go to your accountant for that! I am writing to broaden your perspective on the art of success and prosperity. Being successful and prosperous is an art and a living spiritual law. Those who understand this art more often than not are rich and those who don't have financial struggles.

For the sake of simplicity, I will break this discussion into two parts. The first part is success as an art. The second part is looking at the principles and spiritual dynamics which govern success, prosperity and finances.

I can already sense the resistance in some of you as you begin to read this. I know this first hand. I have been a Pastor for over twenty years, yet I can count sermons I have ever preached on success, prosperity and finances on one hand. The general attitude is that if a preacher talks about prosperity it is because it is assumed, they want your money.

As a result, our natural tendency is to shut off whenever there is a money, success or prosperity talk. People are right to feel so because a lot of preachers have abused this privilege for their own gain.

To this effect I have found myself avoiding the topic about money, success and prosperity all together. I didn't want to be lumped with the usual stereotypes that come with talking about money, success and prosperity.

So why am I breaking the drought and writing about money, success and prosperity? Well, if you believe that knowledge is power, then I want to give you that power to be able to live according to your God-given potential and capacity to succeed and prosper. I can just pray with you about your struggles, or I can also share with you some tools that will enable you to soar above your struggles. I have found that by not teaching about success, prosperity and finances, I am failing to empower people to unlock their God-given potential. If you can't prosper, you can't be a blessing!

Chapter One

MENTAL ATTITUDE

IF you picked up this book, I assume that you want to learn about the secrets in the art of success. By choosing to invest in yourself through reading and educating yourself, I would say the battle is half won already.

You can't do what you have always done and expect a different result. Nowhere is this truer than in dealing with success and prosperity. Your mental attitude sets a trajectory for your prosperity and financial outcome. In order to plot a different trajectory in your finances, you must adjust your thinking and belief system.

If you are ever going to have any discernible change and breakthrough in your finances, the number one thing that needs to change is your attitude and mindset. Don't filter your attitude towards money through the lenses of people, bad behaviour and negativity. Rather unlock your world view and perspective about money to enable you to live an empowered life in the area of prosperity, success and finances.

YOUR GREATEST ASSET

In the words of Napoleon Hill, "Think and Grow Rich." Your mind is your greatest asset. The only limitation you have is your own imagination. Everything you see around you came as a result of someone's imagination. Imagination is the first step to creation. Whatever you allow yourself to think or imagine you can create or become. You are a product of your thoughts and imagination.

If you don't like what you see or where you are, change your thinking! Your life will reflect whatever is in your mind. Your character is fashioned after your mental attitude. To this effect I would say, 'Stop poisoning your mind.' Don't entertain thoughts which are contrary to your objectives.

> ***"Never doubt God's mighty power to work in you and accomplish all this. He will achieve infinitely more than your greatest request, your most unbelievable dream, and exceed your wildest imagination! He will outdo them all, for his miraculous power constantly energizes you."***
> ~ Ephesians 3:20 TPT

JUST IMAGINE

It's an amazing thing that God wants your imagination to run wild because his heart for you is to exceed your wildest imagination. The bigger the dream, the more material God must work with. You provide the dreams and God will provide the capacity. Don't think small, you were created by an omnipotent God for a great purpose.

Small thinking falls far too short of the grand scheme of what you were born for. You are here to serve a great purpose which requires your mind to be unchained and to have a great capacity to dream and imagine BIG.

Don't be afraid to dream. I know a lot of us are gun-shy because the last time we tried, things didn't really workout as we hoped. We were left with a sense of failure and disappointment.

A lack of result does not mean we are failures, it just means we must try things a different way. If at first you don't succeed, try again! The Bible says that, **"Seven times a righteous man may fall and seven times he will rise again."** You only fail when you stop trying. So, your last deal didn't work out? So what? Get up and try again. SETBACKS ARE SETUPS FOR SOMETHING FAR GREATER!

SETBACKS ARE SETUPS

> ***"For the lovers of God may suffer adversity and stumble seven times, but they will continue to***

rise over and over again. But the unrighteous are brought down by just one calamity and will never be able to rise again." ~ Proverbs 24:16 TPT

You have a great God that resides inside you, that means that you have infinite potential and ability to succeed, prosper and create wealth or whatever you set your mind on. For goodness sake! You have the mind of Christ! ***"For, "Who has known the mind of the Lord so as to instruct him?" But we have the mind of Christ."*** ~ 1 Corinthians 2:16 NIV

If that's the case, why then do you shy back from the fullness of your potential? What's holding you back? Is it fear of failure or a sense of inadequacy?

I found this encouragement from Marianne Williamson in her book, **"A Return to Love"**: *"Our deepest fear is not that we are inadequate. Our deepest fear is that we are powerful beyond measure. It is our light, not our darkness that most frightens us. We ask ourselves, who am I to be brilliant, gorgeous, talented, and fabulous?*

Who are you not to be? You are a child of God. You're playing small does not serve the world. There is nothing enlightened about shrinking so that other people will not feel insecure around you. We are all meant to shine, as children do. We were born to make manifest the glory of God that is within us. It is not just in some of us; it is in everyone and as we let our own light shine, we unconsciously give others permission to do the same. As we are liberated from our own fear, our presence automatically liberates others."

Believe in yourself and the dreams God has put in you. If you don't, no one will. God expects a return on his investment in you. There is an exceeding greatness within you because the GREAT I-AM lives within you. Believing in yourself is a big component of trusting God. If you believe that God is true to His word, ways and character then you must believe that you are who God says you are and can do what he says you can.

Paul said, ***"Whatever I have, wherever I am, I can make it through anything in the One who makes me who I am"*** ~ Philippians 4:13 MSG.

WHAT IS YOUR MENTAL ATTITUDE TOWARDS MONEY?

Needless to say, most people have a very poor relationship with money. We are after money for what we can buy with it. This is a typical consumer attitude, using money to meet our current needs!

What if you *grew* your money to meet your future needs? You have heard the saying, "Money doesn't grow on trees!" What if it did? All you must do is to get a money tree seed and plant it in the best soil you can find and water it.

Would you like to know a secret? **Money DOES grow on trees!** Every dollar has a money tree seed inside it. The difference by the end of the day is whether you choose to cook and eat the seed or plant the seed. This also means that every dollar you ever spent had a seed in it. You could say, "That wasn't much money, what could I have done with it?" Well! Like I said before, "Your imagination is your only limitation." We will pick up on this discussion later in the book. But first let's deal with the mental attitudes not conducive for money making. I mean the blockages which prevent you from succeeding in your God given talents.

Chapter Two

Our Belief Systems

OUR belief systems play an integral role in our ability to succeed. Beliefs influence how we see and interact with the world around us. Your life is a manifestation of your core beliefs.

If you believe in incarnation, that what you do in this life will affect who you become in your next life, then you will pay close attention to how you live your life today. If you believe in the law of karma, you are more likely to be more cautious on how you relate and treat other people.

Regardless of our beliefs, we all have to develop the art of forming healthy relationships, becoming mature and whole in our thinking. Let me start by something most people relate to ~ how we relate to money.

Have you heard the saying that, **"The Rich get Richer and the Poor get Poorer?"** There are definitely more reasons to this. But one of the reasons is that the Rich think and believe differently to the poor. Most of us believe that money is the root to all evil. This is a misquotation of the scripture: ***"For the love of money is a root of all kinds of evil. Some people, eager for money, have wandered from the faith and pierced themselves with many griefs."*** ~ 1 Timothy 6:10 NIV

The Passion Translation puts it this way: ***"Loving money is the first step toward all kinds of trouble. Some people run after it so much that they have given up their faith and have turned from Christ –and they will live to regret it.***

Craving more money pushes them away from the faith into error, compounding misery in their lives!" ~ 1 Timothy 6:10 TPT

THE HYPOCRISY OF POVERTY

Indeed, the LOVE of money is the root to all kinds of evil. But money can be a tool for all kinds of good works. If you believe that money is evil and the pursuit of money is ungodly, then you won't have that inner drive and motivation to make money.

The hypocrisy of this attitude is embedded in the fact that most of us get up every morning and go to work to earn a living. We miss the development of inner wealth, of building a legacy when pursuing riches becomes a priority.

Someone once made a snivelling remark to me. He said, "I am happy and content with my life, I don't need wealth and I have no desire to buy houses." I knew this was directed at me because I have a few houses. There is nothing wrong with contentment, it's a Biblical virtue we should all aspire to. But, if we *believe* that we were put on God's earth for something greater than ourselves, then we owe it to the world to be the best that we can be. We owe it to our children and children's children to leave a legacy that would define their world.

We often make fun of rich kids as the "Trust Fund Brigade," or "Born with a silver spoon in their mouths". Maybe it's because with every dollar their parents ever made, they thought past themselves to future generations!

You are here for a greater cause larger than yourself. Therefore, God put an infinite capacity in you in order to meet His demand and expectation of you: ***"But the servant who does not know his master's will and unwittingly does what is wrong will be punished less severely.***

For those who have received a greater revelation from their master are required a greater obedience.

And those who have been entrusted with great responsibility will be held more responsible to their master." ~ Luke 12:48 TPT

If you prefer it in a more traditional sense, here is the scripture in the NIV version of the bible:

"But the one who does not know and does things deserving punishment will be beaten with few blows.

From everyone who has been given much, much will be demanded; and from the one who has been entrusted with much, much more will be asked". ~ Luke 12:48 NIV

The truth is that most people are indifferent in their attitude and beliefs towards money and wealth because of their limited perspectives. We resent people with money and wealth. There is a general sense that the rich rip-off people and steal opportunities from everyone else. We look at wealth as a big pie and the rich people got every piece of the pie and there is nothing left for the rest of us. Generalization can keep you poor!

On the contrary! If you believe Philippians 4:19: ***"I am convinced that my God shall fully satisfy every need you have, for I have seen the abundant riches of glory revealed to me through the Anointed One, Jesus Christ!"*** ~ TPT

THE PIE OR THE RIVER

The riches of God are inexhaustible. Rather than looking at wealth as a pie, I look at wealth as a river. It keeps flowing with no end in sight.

We are all entitled to get our own vessel and draw from this river. The difference is in what vessel we choose to use to draw from this endless river. Some people use a spoon, others use a cup, yet others use a bucket and then there are those who choose to use truck loads or better still put a pump in the river to have a continuous supply to fill up your reservoir. This is the scriptural concept of John 15:5. ***"I am the sprouting vine and you're my branches. As you live in union with me as your source, fruitfulness will stream from within you–but when you live separated from me you are powerless."*** ~ TPT

I had to deal with my own indifference towards wealth and rich people. I am born and raised in Africa where everyone I know is poor. Did you know that in 2016 in the USA alone people spent USD 66.75-billion on pets? In the same year the GDP of Zambia my birth country was USD 20.95-billion. The total combined GDP of Sub-Saharan Africa in 2016 was USD 1.513-trillion. This is the combined GDP of 48 countries. This represents a population of 1.033-billion people.

Comparably, Australia with a population of about 24.6-million people had a GDP of USD 1.69-trillion. Australians spend USD 9.26-billion on pets. What we spend on our pets in the western countries is more than what most countries spend to feed the whole population of people. It's hard to imagine that our pets have such great comforts that millions of people around the world can only dream of.

What am I saying? The disparities between the rich and the poor are undeniable. But if we are to narrow the gap of these disparities, we will need to reconstruct our thinking and belief systems. The communists tried to take from the rich to give to the poor but that never worked out that great because the problem has never been the "lack of" but rather what people do or don't do with what has been entrusted to them. For example, the Zambian government sold a copper mine to a foreign owned company for USD 25-million because they believed they couldn't afford to run the mine. Within three months the new owners made USD 35-million from the same mine. **If there was poverty, it was in their minds not in the lack of resources.**

REALITY OF FAITH

For posterity I am not just talking about positive thinking. I am asking you to start *believing* in the person God made you to be. Begin to *see* yourself as God sees you. Let your mind be *permeated* with the mind of Christ. Take a seat on the heavenly balcony and take in God's view and perspective on life.

> ***"Yes, feast on all the treasures of the heavenly realm and fill your thoughts with heavenly realities, and not with the distractions of the natural realm."*** ~ Colossians 3:2 TPT

It's easy to allow our lives to be led by circumstances and the realities of our everyday pressures. But what if our lives were led by God's reality? That's just it! God wants to bring our minds above our circumstances so we can live above and not beneath. To be the head and not the tail. It all begins by changing mindsets and beliefs.

"Stop imitating the ideals and opinions of the culture around you but be inwardly transformed

by the Holy Spirit through a total reformation of how you think. This will empower you to discern God's will as you live a beautiful life, satisfying and perfect in his eyes." ~ Romans 12:2 TPT

GROW WHAT YOU PLANT

External forces may have an influence on our lives. But live and make choices and decisions out of what God has put in you. Our actions are a fruit of our thoughts and beliefs. Both poverty and wealth are in your mind, which ever one you feed is what will grow and manifest.

I was raised Catholic where people make a vow of poverty in order to serve God! A lot of us live with a poverty mentality in the guise of spirituality. The Lord Jesus taught a lot about denying one's self but never about making an allegiance with the spirit of poverty. You make an allegiance with the Lamb; all we are and have is his. If we have riches, we are merely stewards. It's about our willingness to live for HIM and serve HIM with our entire being and substance.

"Then Jesus said to his disciples, "If you truly want to follow me, you should at once completely reject and disown your own life. And you must be willing to share my cross and experience it as your own, as you continually surrender to my ways.

For if you choose self-sacrifice and lose your lives for my glory, you will continually discover true life. But if you choose to keep your lives for yourselves, you will forfeit what you try to keep.

For even if you were to gain all the wealth and power of this world with everything it could offer you–at the cost of your own life–what good would that be? And what could be more valuable to you than your own soul?" ~ Matthew 16:24-26 TPT

I can hear some people asking, "What about the rich young ruler Jesus told to go and sell everything he owned?" I am glad you asked! ***"As Jesus started on his way, a man came running up to him. Kneeling in front of him, he cried out, "Good Teacher, what one thing am I required to do to gain eternal life?" Jesus responded, "Why do you call me good? Only God is truly good.***

You already know the commandments: 'Do not murder, do not commit adultery, do not steal, do not give a false testimony, do not cheat, and honor your father and mother.'" The man said to Jesus, "Teacher, I have carefully obeyed these laws since my youth."

Jesus fixed his gaze upon the man, with tender love, and said to him, "Yet there is still one thing in you lacking. Go, sell all that you have and give the money to the poor. Then all your treasure will be in heaven. After you've done this, come back and walk with me."

Completely shocked by Jesus' answer, he turned and walked away very sad, for he was extremely rich. Jesus looked at the faces of his disciples and said, "How hard it is for the wealthy to enter into God's kingdom realm." ~ Mark 10:17-23 TPT

This passage does not teach or imply salvation by works.

This is made clear in Ephesians 2:8 TPT: ***"For it was only through this wonderful grace that we believed in him.***

Nothing we did could ever earn this salvation, for it was the gracious gift from God that brought us to Christ! So, no one will ever be able to boast, for salvation is never a reward for good works or human striving."

The gospel according to Matthew gives another perspective on this event: ***"But I've always obeyed every one of them without fail," the young man replied. "What else do I lack?"***

Jesus said to him, "If you really want to be perfect, go immediately and sell everything you own.

Give all your money to the poor and your treasure will be transferred into heaven.

Then come back and follow me for the rest of your life." ~ Matthew 19:16-17 TPT

The young man wanted to know what he needed to do in order to be PERFECT! The Greek word used for the term **"Perfect"** is **"Goal"**. There is no way this man or any other man rich or poor could ever attain this goal by observing the law.

This is the expression in the book of Romans: ***"For by the merit of observing the law no one earns the status of being declared righteous before God, for it is the law that fully exposes and unmasks the reality of sin."*** ~ Romans 3:20 TPT

The rich young ruler desired the right thing. He asked for something Jesus could not give until the day he hung on the cross in an incredible act of divine exchange. On that cross he traded our imperfection for his perfection, our unrighteousness for his righteousness. On that cross he exchanged your poverty for his riches. ***"For you have experienced the extravagant grace of our Lord Jesus Christ, that although he was infinitely rich, he impoverished himself for our sake, so that by his poverty, we could become rich beyond measure."*** ~ 2 Corinthians 8:9 TPT

Paul here is not talking about spiritual riches. Actually, in the entire Chapters 8 and 9, Paul is praising the Church in Corinth for their substantial and generous giving. I would say that there was great wealth among the believers that they were able to meet Paul's challenge in meeting the needs of the famine impoverished Church both in

Macedonia and Jerusalem. Out of the wealth and generosity of the believers came the first ever recorded humanitarian effort to save thousands of people from dying of starvation.

This is the sense of community we see in Acts 4:32-37 TPT: ***"All the believers were one in mind and heart. Selfishness was not a part of their community, for they shared everything they had with one another.***

The apostles gave powerful testimonies about the resurrection of the Lord Jesus, and great measures of grace rested upon them all.

Some who owned houses or land sold them and brought the proceeds before the apostles to distribute to those without. Not a single person among them was needy.

For example, there was a Levite from Cyprus named Joseph, who sold his farmland and placed the proceeds at the feet of the apostles. They nicknamed him Barnabas (or "Encourager")."

People sold their homes and gave the proceeds to the work of the kingdom not because they **had to**, but because they **wanted to!**

THE IDOL OF MONEY

As for Ananias and Sapphira in the next verse their guilt was not that they kept some proceeds for themselves. This couple was judged for lying about the price. All they had to do was simply say, "We have sold our property; we will give some money to the work and keep the rest for ourselves!" This is what Zacchaeus did! ***"Zacchaeus joyously welcomed Jesus and was amazed over his gracious visit to his home. Zacchaeus stood in front of the Lord and said, "Half of all that I own I will give to the poor. And Lord, if I have cheated anyone, I promise to pay back four times as much as I stole."*** ~ Luke 19:8 TPT

Jesus responds to Zacchaeus by saying, ***"This shows that today life has come to you and your household, for you are a true son of Abraham. The Son of Man has come to seek out and to give life to those who are lost."*** ~ Luke 19:9-10 TPT

Jesus didn't say, "Hey Zacch! What about the other half?" It had become clearly apparent that money was no longer an idol or a snare in Zacchaeus' heart.

For the rich young man this was a severe test of values. Would he value Jesus above his earthly possessions? Did he truly love his neighbor as himself like he claimed? The answer was no, **he had set his *wealth* as an *idol* in his heart.** Contrary to his claim the man broke the first commandment, ***"You shall have no other gods before Me."*** Jesus tested the man to reveal what was in his heart. Jesus is our greatest reward; he is the one we seek and pursue. Wealth is a byproduct of our stewardship and dedicated service to Him by serving the needs of His people. I will talk more about this in the chapter, The Art of Success.

All things considered; I would have loved to have been Joseph of Arimathea. A wealthy man who loved Jesus and had the privilege of paying for the burial of the Lord Jesus and provide a tomb to lay his body. I wonder what would have happened if our Lord didn't have some wealthy and influential followers like Joseph?

I have taken a bit of time on this subject because I am sick and tired of hearing people misinterpret scripture to justify poverty mentalities, more especially people in ministry.

I have always been inspired by the Apostle Paul's resourcefulness and entrepreneur skills in his tent-making business.

KNOWN BY THE FRUIT

So, how do we know what is in us? Look at the fruit in your life! Jesus said, ***"People are known in this same way. Out of the virtue stored in their hearts, good and upright people will produce good fruit.***

But out of the evil hidden in their hearts, evil ones will produce what is evil.

For the overflow of what has been stored in your heart will be seen by your fruit and will be heard in your words." ~ Luke 6:45 TPT

Let his truth manifest in you and through you. Turn a leaf in your thinking, attitudes and beliefs on finances, I guarantee you will experience a change in your finances. ***"Everyone who hears my teaching and applies it to his life can be compared to a wise man who built his house on an unshakable foundation.***

When the rains fell and the flood came, with fierce winds beating upon his house, it stood firm because of its strong foundation.

But everyone who hears my teaching and does not apply it to his life can be compared to a foolish man who built his house on sand. When it rained and rained and the flood came, with wind and waves beating upon his house, it collapsed and was swept away." ~ Matthew 7:24-27 TPT

Chapter Three

The Power of Spoken Words

"The Holy Spirit is the one who gives life, that which is of the natural realm is of no help. The words I speak to you are Spirit and life. But there are still some of you who won't believe."
~ John 6:63 TPT

WORDS have power to build or destroy. With your words you can create a beautiful world around you or tear down, you can bring hope, encouragement and inspiration.

The secret is in what words *you choose* to speak. With words God created the entire universe both seen and unseen out of nothing. "Let there be light" and suddenly out of the great depth of darkness light emerged. The word of God is spirit and life.

Hebrews 4:12 says that ***"The word of God is living and active"***. Perhaps the greatest marvel in all creation is that God created you and me in His own image and likeness. We were created to mirror and reflect Him in all His glory and fullness: ***"Then God said, "Let us make mankind in our image, in our likeness, so that they may rule over the fish in the sea and the birds in the sky, over the livestock and all the wild animals, and over all the creatures that move along the ground."*** ~ Genesis 1:26 NIV

We were created to mirror and reflect Him in all His glory and fullness. ***"We can all draw close to him with the veil removed from our faces. And with no veil we all become like mirrors who brightly reflect the glory of the Lord Jesus.***

We are being transfigured into his very image as we move from one brighter level of glory to another.

And this glorious transfiguration comes from the Lord, who is the Spirit." ~ 2 Corinthians 3:18 TPT

Now that we have established that you were made with God's creative power and ability in you. **What are you creating with your words?** You were created to co-create and reign with your heavenly Father. In as much as your thoughts and mental attitude impacts who you are, as a man thinks so he is! Your words impact what you and the atmosphere around you becomes. When you speak, you release the creative power of words. ***"That's what the Scripture means when it says: "I have made you the father of many nations."***

He is our example and father, for in God's presence he believed that God can raise the dead and CALL INTO BEING THINGS THAT DON'T EVEN EXIST YET." ~ Romans 4:17 TPT.

Train yourself to call forth life and speak God's word into your finances and your everyday circumstances. Let God's truth be your confession. Declare what God's word says and not what you feel or see. Keep believing and your feelings and present reality will catch up with God's reality for you.

Faith is what we do while we are waiting for the manifestation of God's promises in our lives. It's the ability to hold on when we cannot yet see the path forward. The word of God becomes our life flow. Like Ezekiel, learn to speak to the dry bones. Declare and prophesy and see the impossible become possible, the immovable object move, and the valley of dry bones become a great army.

With your words, sow seeds of faith not doubt, sow seeds of life not death. Take a walk and have a talk with those intimidating giants in your life. Declare to them what God says! ***"Then he said to me, "Prophesy to these bones and say to them, 'Dry bones, hear the word of the Lord! This is what the Sovereign Lord says to these bones: I will make breath enter you, and you will come to life. I will attach tendons to you and make flesh come upon you and cover you with skin; I will put breath in you, and you will come to life. Then you will know that I am the Lord.'"***

So, I prophesied as I was commanded. And as I was prophesying, there was a noise, a rattling sound, and the bones came together, bone to bone.

I looked, and tendons and flesh appeared on them and skin covered them, but there was no breath in them.

Then he said to me, "Prophesy to the breath; prophesy, son of man, and say to it, 'This is what the Sovereign Lord says: Come, breath, from the four winds and breathe into these slain, that they may live.'"

So, I prophesied as he commanded me, and breath entered them; they came to life and stood up on their feet–a vast army." ~ Ezekiel 37:4-10 NIV

What are you releasing with your words? ***"Receive this truth: Whatever you forbid on earth will be considered to be forbidden in heaven, and whatever you release on earth will be considered to be released in heaven."*** ~ Matthew 18:18 TPT.

Nothing happens on earth unless you allow it to happen. What are you allowing to happen in your area of influence? What you speak and agree with is what you will become.

Throughout scripture and history, whenever God needed to bring change to a community, He would send a prophet to declare His word. This is a wonderful picture of God partnering and co-creating with His people. The Roman centurion understood the power of words and authority. Jesus didn't need to go to his house to heal his servant. All Jesus had to do was speak the word. Sometimes all you need to do is speak the word. ***"But the Roman officer interjected, "Lord, who am I to have you come into my house? I understand your authority for I too am a man who walks under authority and have authority over soldiers who serve under me.***

I can tell one to go and he'll go, and another to come and he'll come. I order my servants and they'll do whatever I ask.

So, I know that all you need to do is to stand here and command healing over my son and he will be instantly healed." ~ Matthew 8:8-9 TPT

I am not talking about "name it and claim it". I am talking about aligning your heart with God's heart where His truth becomes your truth. It's about rejecting and overcoming all the lies which prevent you from being prosperous as God intends for you to be.

Let your words shift atmospheres and pave paths in the jungles of pessimism and negativity, because deep in your heart you believe, that with God all things are possible!

> ***"Jesus looked at them and said, "With man this is impossible, but with God all things are possible."***
> ~ Matthew 19:26 NIV

Chapter Four

The Human Blueprints

BLUEPRINTS are a reproduction of technical drawings and documents outlining the design and architecture of a product. When we look at these blueprints, we begin to understand the make-up and the process assembly. We become intimately acquainted with every component of the design, function and purpose. The blueprints reveal how a product was designed and meant to function.

When it came to the "assembly" of man, God the master builder used the same design and "production process". He made blueprints for man!

First, God designed man with a very clear outline of what he was to look like. Second, God stipulated the function and purpose of man. Lastly, He published a user-manual explaining how everything works, the Bible.

On day-six of creation God was about to make something like nothing He had ever made before. In five days of creating, God made everything and the entire universe as we know it without a board meeting or consultation. But on the sixth day in Genesis 1:26 God convened a board meeting. This was a high level meeting attended by God the Father, the Son and the Holy Spirit. Here is a preview of the proceedings at this trinitarian board meeting. ***"Then God said, "Let us make mankind in our image, in our likeness, so that they may rule over the fish in the sea and the birds in the sky, over the livestock and all the wild animals, and over all the creatures that move along the ground."*** ~ Genesis 1:26 NIV

God expresses His desire to make an exceptional being like nothing He has made so far called ADAM ~ the Hebrew root word means "ruddy" ~ to show blood in the face, to flush or turn rosy.

Design point number one ~ this Adam, though a species, was to have a unique personality and individuality.

He was to be "ruddy", healthy and cheerful with a good-looking face. This is the word used to describe young David in 1 Samuel 16:12: ***"So he sent for him and had him brought in. He was glowing with health and had a fine appearance and handsome features."*** NIV

In this design concept man had to have a distinct face as a mark of his personality and individuality in order to uniquely interface and interact with God and all creation.

Design point number two ~ Man was to be made in the image of the Father, Son and Holy Spirit. You were not just made in the image of God but the image of the trinity.

The word "image" speaks of a representative figure and is used sixteen times in the Old Testament. Five of those refer to man. This means that the design and architectural make up of man was to represent and reflect the exact nature and appearance of the trinity.

Other instances where the word image is used in the Bible refers to the making of an IDOL. God made an idol of Himself in man. Therefore, God is so obsessed with you because you are the idol in His heart. Consequently, you are not allowed to make an idol to represent Him because He has got *you* for that! Remember John 14:9 ***"Philip, I've been with you all this time and you still don't know who I am? How could you ask me to show you the Father, for anyone who has looked at me has seen the Father."*** TPT

In this design concept of man, God is taking the blueprints of His own architectural design, to make an idol of Himself as a representation to all creation of what God is like.

Design point number three ~ God wants to make man not just in His image but also in His likeness.

The other descriptive word for LIKENESS in this Bible text is MODEL. A model is a three-dimensional representation of an object, person or a proposed structure, typically on a smaller scale than the original. Man was to be an exact replica of God Himself. Likeness speaks of the resemblance and similarities. Man was to be similar to God in design, function and purpose.

In this design concept of man, God is taking the blueprints of His own architectural design, function and purpose to recreate Himself in a smaller scale while preserving the design integrity.

Design point number four ~ God wanted to make a male and female version of man to co-exist in a symphony of partnership, fellowship and oneness.

"So, God created mankind in his own image, in the image of God he created them; male and female he created them." Genesis 1:27 NIV

PURPOSE AND FUNCTION

> ***"God blessed them and said to them, "Be fruitful and increase in number; fill the earth and subdue it.***

> ***Rule over the fish in the sea and the birds in the sky and over every living creature that moves on the ground."***
>
> ***Then God said, "I give you every seed-bearing plant on the face of the whole earth and every tree that has fruit with seed in it. They will be yours for food."***
>
> Genesis 1:26-29 NIV

In the scripture above, God reveals the purpose and function of man. God outlines four aspects of human existence. God blessed you to be fruitful, multiply, and increase and to have dominion: ***"The heavens belong to our God; they are his alone, but he has given us the earth and put us in charge."*** ~ Psalm 115:16 TPT.

It's amazing to think that God gave you dominion over the earth, to rule and administer heaven on earth on His behalf. God has got great confidence in your ability to perform this task because He made you like Himself. You are qualified by design, you were made to be fruitful, multiply and rule. For as long as you look to God and walk in His ways you will prosper and never fail.

David in Psalm 23:1-6 had this to say, ***"The Lord is my best friend and my shepherd. I always have more than enough.***

He offers a resting place for me in his luxurious love. His tracks take me to an oasis of peace, the quiet brook of bliss. That's where he restores and revives my life.

He opens before me pathways to God's pleasure and leads me along in his footsteps of righteousness so that I can bring honor to his name.

Lord, even when your path takes me through the valley of deepest darkness, fear will never conquer me, for you already have! You remain close to me and lead me through it all the way.

Your authority is my strength and my peace. The comfort of your love takes away my fear. I'll never be lonely, for you are near.

You become my delicious feast even when my enemies dare to fight.

You anoint me with the fragrance of your Holy Spirit; you give me all I can drink of you until my heart overflows.

So why would I fear the future? For your goodness and love pursue me all the days of my life.

Then afterward, when my life is through, I'll return to your glorious presence to be forever with you!" TPT

When your confidence is in God your maker, the Bible declares that you will never be put to shame! ***"Those who look to him are radiant; their faces are never covered with shame."*** ~ Psalm 34:5 NIV

Not only did God make you to rule and have dominion, He also made you to represent Him. Consider this, ***"We're Christ's representatives. God uses us to persuade men and women to drop their differences and enter God's work of making things right between them.***

We're speaking for Christ himself now: Become friends with God; he's already a friend with you." ~ 2 Corinthians 5:20 MSG

God didn't just make you like Himself in His image and likeness, He also deposited a part of Himself in you by His Holy Spirit! You are Him and one with Him in Christ Jesus.

God's power works in and through you! How much power you say? Explosive power! The power defined in Greek as "DUNAMIS."

YOU ARE ABLE AND CAPABLE

> ***"But I promise you this–the Holy Spirit will come upon you and you will be filled with power.***
>
> ***And you will be my messengers to Jerusalem, throughout Judea, the distant provinces –even to the remotest places on earth!"*** ~ Acts 1:8 TPT

This is the most incredible upgrade to humanity in all human history. The word "power" in the scripture above is the Greek word *"dunamis"* I mentioned earlier. This is where we get the word **"Dynamite"** or **"Dynamo"** from. Dynamo as in the electrical generator which creates direct current using a commutator.

In essence, with regards to Acts 1:8, it means to have the ability, abundance and strength.

It is inherent power which enables you to perform beyond your human capacity. It transforms you into a miracle worker which is a miracle in itself. Literally by the Holy Spirit, you are more than any comic hero character. You are the real Superman or Wonder Woman.

AN AMBASSADOR OF THE KING

Now then, why did God offer you his Spirit? So that you can be His messenger and represent Him effectively. You are the Messenger and Ambassador of the Kingdom of God.

If a messenger, what message do you bring? If an ambassador, how well do you represent the majesty of God and His Kingdom in glory, power, wholeness, fruitfulness, character, wealth and prosperity? I have never seen the Ambassador of the United States of America in any country even the remotest and poorest of them all live in poverty and drive a beat-up car. Go to the poorest country and visit the US embassy. It will stand out like an Oasis in the desert! But you and I represent someone and a Kingdom far greater, but, in many instances, we have become the definition of poverty and failure. I think it's about time this wrong was rewritten, what do you think?

According to the Strongs Concordance, here are some Verbs of "Dunamis":

~ **dunatós** (1415) which means one who has an ability. This is you, right?

~ **dúnamai** (1410) ~ to be able. Yes, indeed you are! God has made you able by His Spirit.

~ **dunatéō** (1414) To have great ability. This is the word used in 2 Corinthians 13:3: ***"I will give you all the proof you want that Christ speaks through me. Christ is not weak when he deals with you; he is powerful among you."*** NLT.

The passion Translation says that Christ is powerful within you. ***"Since you are demanding proof that the Anointed One is speaking through me, I will give you proof by exercising discipline among you.***

For just as I told you the last time I was there–and now, though absent, I say it again–that when I come, I will not go easy on those whom I've already warned and those who continue to persist in their sin.

Christ is not weak or feeble in his dealings with you but mighty and powerful within you." ~ 2 Corinthians 13:3 TPT.

~ **dunamóō** (1412) and **endunamóō** (1743) ~ to strengthen.

These are the words we find in Colossians 1:11 TPT: ***"And we pray that you would be energized with all his explosive power from the realm of his magnificent glory, filling you with great hope."*** How amazing is this!

The Strongs Concordance also gives us a Noun of Dunamis;

First things first, what is a noun? I am glad you asked! It's a word used to identify any class of people, places and objects. The noun in this event is ***dunástēs*** which speaks of someone who exercises dominion authority. You get to look at yourself through Acts 1:8 in a whole new light. This is the basic concept of what we know as a **Dynasty**.

Remember the purpose and function of man is to be fruitful, multiply and increase in number. This means that you and your class or offspring if you like, are expected to become a dynasty, an empire and a great nation. These are the premises of Genesis 12:2, ***"I will make you into a great nation. I will bless you and make you famous, and you will be a blessing to others."*** NLT.

This is what makes a ***DYNASTY*** a realm of authority and influence passed on from generation to generation. The sun is never meant to set on your legacy when you die.

Reputation and good deeds may be forgotten but your dynasty will endure like a monument for many generations yet unborn to see and experience.

I never met Mr. Henry Ford, but I sure know a Ford motor vehicle when I see one. This is all part and parcel of what God made you to be.

"But remember the LORD your God, for it is he who gives you the ability to produce wealth, and so confirms his covenant, which he swore to your forefathers, as it is today." Deuteronomy 8:18 NIV

You have the inherent power of the Almighty God residing in you by virtue of your nature by being His Child. You were designed to carry the Glory of God and to exert His power and influence by exercising dominion and authority over all creation. You are an emitter of God's wealth-creating power!

Your dynasty reflects God's heart for nation building. God's desire has always been to raise people, a nation or a community of people through which He would reflect His nature and ways. Therefore, God raised the Nation of Israel in the Bible. They were to showcase the glory, wisdom and splendour of the Maker of Heaven and Earth. That is an extraordinary responsibility and privilege. This is what we read in Deuteronomy 4:5-8 NLT: ***"Look, I now teach you these decrees and regulations just as the Lord my God commanded me, so that you may obey them in the land you are about to enter and occupy.***

Obey them completely, and you will display your wisdom and intelligence among the surrounding nations.

When they hear all these decrees, they will exclaim, 'How wise and prudent are the people of this great nation!' For what great nation has a god as near to them as the Lord our God is near to us whenever we call on him?

And what great nation has decrees and regulations as righteous and fair as this body of instructions that I am giving you today?"

We reflect God our Father as His Glory shines through the prism of our lives for the people around us to see the magnificence of his majesty.

1 Peter 2:9 sums up my thoughts, ***"But you are God's chosen treasure –priests who are kings, a spiritual "nation" set apart as God's devoted ones.***

He called you out of darkness to experience his marvelous light, and now he claims you as his very own.

He did this so that you would broadcast his glorious wonders throughout the world." TPT

All that is left for you to do is go and be what you were designed and made for, BE FRUITFUL, MULTIPLY, INCREASE and HAVE DOMINION In all that you do!

Please if you agree say AMEN!

Chapter Five

BORN TO PROSPER

APATHY and complacency are unnatural for human beings. It is our genetic make up to desire and pursue more of everything. We have an inbuilt God-given capacity within us to increase, multiply and prosper. We were made to prosper and continually grow in both riches and wealth.

However, by pursuing the greatness within us without a divine connection to our purpose and existence we become greedy and expose ourselves to the spirit of Mammon. Instead of money being a tool for all kinds of good, we become slaves to money.

The key to unleashing the greatness within you is to become better at being who you were born to be and effective in living out your purpose. If you can be better and effective, fruitfulness is a mere natural by-product.

Most people try to be like their heroes, this is futile! The best person you can ever be is the person you were born to be. Embrace who you are and learn to better and harness the skills, abilities and gifting God has given you. If all God requires and expects from each one of us is to bear fruit in accordance with the seed, He has vested in us, then it is impossible to fail. In other words, God is not asking any of us to do something He has not given us the ability and capacity to do.

We should aim at being the best version of who we are and dispense our purpose with a spirit of excellence. This is what will be our distinguishing mark and separate us from the pack.

The bible talks about Daniel. He was distinguished by the spirit of excellence which was on him. When we are better and effective at being who we are, we will be abundantly fruitful.

You were created not just to bear fruit, but much fruit. **You were born for the "above and beyond, headship not the tail."**

But if we are to prosper and better ourselves, we need to understand who we are and God's purpose in and through us. We must know what God thinks and says about us. Nothing spells out what God intended for you to be better than the scriptures. Here is His master plan for us in Genesis 1:28-29 NLT: ***"Then God blessed them and said, "Be fruitful and multiply. Fill the earth and govern it.***

Reign over the fish in the sea, the birds in the sky, and all the animals that scurry along the ground."

Then God said, "Look! I have given you every seed-bearing plant throughout the earth and all the fruit trees for your food."

From this passage of scripture allow me to make a few remarks:

1. You Are Blessed

It's incredible that God's first interaction with man was to pronounce a blessing!

The concept of declaring a blessing on people is so dear to God that he even commanded the priests to speak a blessing over His people. ***"Then the Lord said to Moses, "Tell Aaron and his sons to bless the people of Israel with this special blessing: 'May the Lord bless you and protect you. May the Lord smile on you and be gracious to you.***

May the Lord show you his favor and give you his peace.' Whenever Aaron and his sons bless the people of Israel in my name, I myself will bless them." Numbers 6:22-27 NLT

God's desire is to bless you and for you to have a blessed life. The declaration of God's blessing on your life is not just meant to make you feel good about yourself. It affirms who God made you to be and activates His purpose and destiny in you. His blessing unlocks the seed of greatness within you to bring forth much fruit. The blessing of God causes you to prosper. Proverbs 10:22 52 says, ***"The blessing of the Lord makes a person rich, and he adds no sorrow with it."*** NLT

There you go! I have it on good authority that it is not God's intention that we should live with lack and in poverty. You have the Father's favor; His heart is naturally disposed towards you with loving kindness. This means that every time God thinks of you or looks at you, His face radiates with great joy and delight He is so pleased with you.

2. Be Fruitful

When God says be fruitful, we can deduce that you can be fruitful and have the capacity to multiply. If it were not so God would not have asked man to be fruitful. The Bible uses the imagery of bearing fruit a lot in reference to productivity.

One such instance is John 15:1-2 NLT: ***"I am the true grapevine, and my Father is the gardener. He cuts off every branch of mine that doesn't produce fruit, and he prunes the branches that do bear fruit so they will produce even more."***

A fruit is a product of a tree or other plant that contains seed. It is this quality that enables a fruit to replicate itself and keep producing fruit in perpetuity. The implication is that you are a mature tree/branch with the ability to bear fruit. In turn the seed in your fruit will propagate and continue the circle of propagation until the seed in you becomes so vast.

God commands increase and productivity from His seed of fruitfulness passed on from Him to you when He made you in His own image and likeness. The all-sufficient God put His seed of greatness and prosperity inside of you. You were made to increase and were born to prosper in every aspect of life.

You have seed in you to produce fruit for both life and godliness: ***"Everything we could ever need for life and complete devotion to God has already been deposited in us by his divine power.***

For all this was lavished upon us through the rich experience of knowing him who has called us by name and invited us to come to him through a glorious manifestation of his goodness.

As a result of this, he has given you magnificent promises that are beyond all price, so that through the power of these tremendous promises you can experience partnership with the divine nature, by which you have escaped

the corrupt desires that are of the world." 1 Peter 1:3-4 TPT

> ***"Every spiritual blessing in the heavenly realm has already been lavished upon us as a love gift from our wonderful heavenly Father, the Father of our Lord Jesus–all because he sees us wrapped into Christ. Therefore, we celebrate him with all our hearts!"*** Ephesians 1:3 TPT

You are a fruit with a seed in your DNA. The whole purpose and reason for you having seed is to reproduce what God has deposited in you. Fruit that keeps on yielding so that you would never know a day in your life without provision. David said, ***"I was once young, but now I'm old. Not once have I found a lover of God forsaken by him, nor have any of their children gone hungry."*** Psalm 37:25 TPT

Therefore, God gave you the seed because He knows that if you've got the seed, you will never lack, and your children will never go hungry. God confidently gave His word to you when He said, ***"If you listen to these commands of the Lord your***

God that I am giving you today, and if you carefully obey them, the Lord will make you the head and not the tail, and you will always be on top and never at the bottom." Deuteronomy 28:13 NLT. You were born to be on top! ***"This generous God who supplies abundant seed for the farmer, which becomes bread for our meals, is even more extravagant toward you. First, he supplies every need, plus more. Then he multiplies the seed as you sow it, so that the harvest of your generosity will grow."*** 2 Corinthians 9:10 TPT

This is one of my favorite verses. It gives insight into the principles of increase, multiplication and wealth. The idea is not just to meet today's needs, but to make provisions for tomorrow and future generations. Proverbs 13:22 makes this remark, ***"The benevolent man leaves an inheritance that endures to his children's children, but the wealth of the wicked is treasured up for the righteous."*** TPT

God provides for us by giving us seed so we can increase in wealth and riches so we can leave an inheritance for our children's children. We are talking about great wealth to last for generations.

What is the benchmark of God's idea for prosperity? More wealth and resources than you will ever need in your life time. You were not meant to outlive your resources, but your resources are meant to outlast you.

The problem I have discovered is that a lot of people cry out to God for bread. When God gives them seed, they complain because they feel that God didn't answer their prayers because they didn't receive what they asked God for. This is very short sighted; we need to look past today because God has a big picture in mind. Of course, planting the seed and taking care of it until it becomes a tree is a lot of work. Waiting for the tree to bear fruit takes patience. I can see the temptation to take an easy way out to skip the process and just eat the seed. I will talk a little bit more about this in a following chapter, **"Never Eat Your Seed".**

REDEFINING THE PURSUIT OF HAPPINESS

You were born for a purpose. Jeremiah 1:5 says: ***"I knew you before I formed you in your mother's womb.***

Before you were born, I set you apart and appointed you as my prophet to the nations." NLT.

God chose you and assigned you to a role unique and specific to the ability and capacity He has put in you.

The economy of heaven revolves around supplying and providing for God's purposes in you. **The key to fruitfulness is living our lives for the purpose we were born for.** Life is more productive when you function in a role you were born for. Trying to perform outside God's gifting on your life can be equated to using a pair of scissors to mow the lawn. This would be very frustrating and unfruitful, though scissors are a great piece of equipment, they were never designed for mowing the lawn. ***"So we are convinced that every detail of our lives is continually woven together to fit into God's perfect plan of bringing good into our lives, for we are his lovers who have been called to fulfill his designed purpose."*** Romans 8:28 TPT

In the market for a home

I learnt this lesson years ago when we were hoping to buy a house. We had some debts and no savings. All we had was a leading in the Spirit that it was time to buy property as a prophetic act of putting a stake in the ground. We went online to see what was available for sale in our area. Within fifteen minutes we realized that we couldn't afford anything. The bank would not even look at us. I decided it was time to have a serious conversation with God. I reminded Him about all His promises to me and my family, I informed God that He wasn't making a good impression on my kids by not fulfilling His promises.

To my surprise God responded by defending His integrity and position. He said, **"Son, I never promised you a home for your family! I promised you a Ministry Centre."** I clearly understood what God meant, He was committed to meeting my needs by providing for His purposes on my life so I can fulfil the desires of His heart in creating a place where the needs of His people could be met.

Sobered up by the Father's response I proceeded by asking for the budget or price range on this Ministry Centre! My goodness! Was I amazed by Papa God's reply! He said, **"Don't worry about the price, just choose whichever property you like."**

Can you believe this? Father God just handed me a blank check and set me loose on the property market. The only condition was that we pick a property we liked regardless of price. I convened a family meeting and broke the good news. The children began to make a list of features they wanted in the property. There were things like, swimming pool, lots of land to have a horse and ride quad bikes, the wife wanted a creative house with an art studio and her own private jungle, and the list went on. Armed with this list and God's promise of a blank check, we went back property hunting. What a freedom to shop without a budget.

We found the property.

One day I was out doing some routine stuff when I received a phone call from a very excited wife.

The conversation was something like this, *"I have found the property that I like! I just finished inspecting the property and I really like it. Can you hurry down here the agent is waiting to show you the property."* As soon as I could, I was there! It was everything the wife and the kids wished for. The property was coming up for auction in a week. How the auctions work is that you need to have the cash or a bank loan pre-approval in order to register for the auction. You guessed it! We didn't have either, the bank lady gave us some very good advice. She told us to focus on saving for a small house and work our way up to something like the property we were looking at in the future. This was very good advice, but we needed good news.

How time flies, it was already Friday night! The eve of the auction scheduled for Saturday morning and we had nothing, not even $100 in the bank. So, my wife and I decided to go prayer walking on the property just to get a sense of what Papa God was saying. We got to the property and stood by the boundary fence praying up a storm. As soon as we started praying, I had a vision of a lot of cars parked on the street along the boundary fence.

I asked Papa, "Lord what are these cars? Are they cars at the auction tomorrow?" Papa said, *"No Son, these cars belong to parents waiting to pick up their children from the event you are running!"* From that point on, we knew beyond any shadow of a doubt that that property was ours.

The next morning up and early we were at the auction. We had nothing; we couldn't even register for the auction. If the property sold for $50, we wouldn't have been able to buy it. **All we had was God's word.** This was very exciting because we were taking front row seats to watch God perform a miracle. We knew by the time this auction was over the property was ours, but how is he going pull it off? Oh, the intrigue! There were about forty people at the auction. My motto is, ***"Do all the possibilities you can and let God do the impossibilities."*** With this in mind I asked Papa God if there was anything I needed to do. Papa said, "Go and sign your name in the public indemnity/insurance form everybody visiting the property had to sign." He also said, "Write down your offer besides your name and verbally repeat your offer to the real estate agent before the auction begins."

Apparently, my offer was very funny that the agent laughed and said if we ever got the property for what I was offering he would eat his hat! My offer was out by about $300,000 according their valuations.

I didn't let that bother me because I knew what my Heavenly Father said! That was the only thing that mattered. **His promise was a seed we were about to see manifest.** The auction was on. People with the money were bidding. When the biding hit $30,000 from our "ridiculous" offer we saw Heaven step in, and the atmosphere instantly changed. Hard to explain but it was as though everything came to a standstill and no one knew what to do. The auctioneer placed a vendor bid which raised the bid to my offer and within three-minutes everyone cleared out and left the auction.

We stood there in great amazement wondering just what happened? The property was passed, meaning it was not sold at auction. The agent told us to wait so he could consult with the vendor.

Moments later the agent was back. The vendor said she had a New Age belief system and believed in karma, she said to us, 'I don't know what you did in your previous life to deserve this property, but you can have the property for the offer you made'. Because this wasn't the auction conditions for sale, we had 21 days to come up with payment. In less than 21 days we had all the funds for the property come through.

Not only that, we also had our other debts paid out! Now that is my God. This property is now the Centre of Access Church Global and our Charitable organization, Kingdom Resource Network.

This is what I meant when I said that God is moved to work things out for the good of those who are in love with Him. People who have aligned and positioned themselves to fulfill God's purpose in their lives. This redefines our understanding of the pursuit of happiness! **The pursuit of happiness can never be attained by accumulation of wealth but by fulfilling God's purpose in your life.**

TENDING THE SEED OF GOD'S PURPOSE

Ever wondered why so many rich people are miserable and take their own lives? Or are on a spiritual path, "searching"? This is code for "I don't know what on earth I am here for!"

Your focus should never be on making money, but rather on being diligent in cultivating the seed God has invested in you. You need to learn to be a good steward of whatever God has entrusted to you. **Diligence in tending the seed of God's purpose in you will produce enduring fruit.** Stewardship of what God has entrusted to you will yield immense increase and multiplication.

It's not about chasing after wealth and riches; I just want you to understand that wealth and riches are as a result of you being effective at being who God made you to be. He made you to be fruitful, increase, multiply and to have dominion! Here is God's promise to Abraham which is also true for you, ***"I will make you into a great nation. I will bless you and make you famous, and you will be a blessing to others."*** Genesis 12:2 NLT. Your God wants to bless you and make your name great!

God's blessing is not just about you, it's about you being blessed so you can be a blessing to others. You are meant to be blessed so you can be a channel for blessings to flow through.

Wealth is intergenerational, it's meant to be passed on as seed from one generation to another. We were all meant to build our lives on the foundations of our fathers. Let your ceiling be the floor for the next generation.

POVERTY IS A CURSE

> ***"Yet, Christ paid the full price to set us free from the curse of the law. He absorbed it completely as he became a curse in our place. For it is written: "Everyone who is hung upon a tree is doubly cursed."*** Galatians 3:13 TPT.

Jesus' death on the cross was a divine exchange. His life for ours, His status for ours, His blessings for our curses. Jesus is the only person in all human history who was specifically born to be poor and to die, the rest of us were born to live, excel and prosper. Jesus came to correct the errors caused by the fall of Adam and sin. John says that Jesus came that we may have abundant life: ***"A thief has only one thing in mind–he wants to steal, slaughter, and destroy.***

But I have come to give you everything in abundance, more than you expect –life in its fullness until you overflow!" John 10:10 TPT.

Poverty is a byproduct of the fallen state of man. It's not your portion, if Jesus made that exchange for you on that cross! Your poverty for his riches, then it's an error for you to live in poverty: ***"For you have experienced the extravagant grace of our Lord Jesus Christ, that although he was infinitely rich, he impoverished himself for our sake, so that by his poverty, we could become rich beyond measure."*** 2 Corinthians 8:9 TPT.

Chapter Six

Created For Increase

MONEY IS NOT THE ISSUE

In my earlier days of ministry, I was church planting in villages in Africa. Sometimes I would walk 40km/ 25miles a day. The soles of my shoes wore off and I needed a new pair.

I prayed about it asking God to provide some money so I could buy a new pair of shoes. As I was praying asking God for money, He spoke to me by asking a question. **"Son, what do you *need*?"** I responded by saying, "I need a pair of shoes!"

To which the Lord proceeded to say, "So why are you focusing on the money?" **The issues not the money but what you need!**

I learnt something that day which has impacted my whole outlook on provision. Never to make money the issue. Within a couple of days, someone said to me that he had been to Israel and bought this beautiful pair of sandals. The Lord spoke to him to give that pair of Israeli sandals to me. How awesome is that? I ended up with a new pair of shoes far better and superior compared to any I could have ever contemplated buying or were available in any store in Zambia, Africa at the time.

What I learnt is that when we focus on money, we limit our options! God is far greater than the money box. Money is here today and gone tomorrow but God's seed in you will always bring provision. Therefore, ***"God is the one who provides seed for the farmer and then bread to eat. In the same way, he will provide and increase your resources and then produce a great harvest of generosity in you."*** 2 Corinthians 9:10 NLT

GOD'S PRINCIPLE OF SEED MULTIPLICATION

God has got a sustainable approach when it comes to meeting your needs. He gives you seed and then increases your seed so you can have exponential growth of resources and provisions. You were created to excel, increase and multiply. Consider what the bible says about Isaac, ***"The man became rich, and his wealth continued to grow until he became very wealthy."*** Genesis 26:13 NIV. What about his Father Abram? ***"Abram had become very wealthy in livestock and in silver and gold."*** Genesis 13:2 NIV. Let's not forget Jacob in Genesis 30:43 NLT. ***"As a result, Jacob became very wealthy, with large flocks of sheep and goats, female and male servants, and many camels and donkeys."***

There is a pattern here! Three generations with two things in common, great wealth and favor with God. Deuteronomy 8:18 NIV gives some insight. *"**But remember the Lord your God, for it is he who gives you the ability to produce wealth, and so confirms his covenant, which he swore to your ancestors, as it is today."***

What do you have in common with Abraham, Isaac and Jacob? You have the same God. The God who gave them the ability to produce wealth is the same God, He never changes. He still affirms His covenant today by blessing His people. This was true then and is true now.

Why did God make these men wealthy? As a confirmation of His covenant. Which covenant? ***"When Abram was ninety-nine years old, the Lord appeared to him and said, "I am El-Shaddai – 'God Almighty.' Serve me faithfully and live a blameless life. I will make a covenant with you, by which I will guarantee to give you countless descendants."*** Genesis 17:1-2 NLT

All three patriarchs knew God by the name El-Shaddai. El-Shaddai is the term found in the passages that report God's promises of fertility, land, and abundance to them. It indicates that God can fulfill His promises.

"And through your descendants all the nations of the earth will be blessed–all because you have obeyed me." Genesis 22:18 NLT. You share in this blessing. In Christ Jesus you even have a better covenant with God.

BORN TO MULTIPLY

"Be fruitful and multiply." So, say to yourself, **"I am a fruit and there is seed in me."** That's right! Inside you there is seed. Because there is seed in you, you have the ability and the capacity to multiply. Not only do you have the ability and the capacity to multiply, you have the mandate before God to do so. Look at what Jesus said, ***"I am a true sprouting vine, and the farmer who tends the vine is my Father. He cares for the branches connected to me by lifting and propping up the fruitless branches and pruning every fruitful branch to yield a greater harvest."*** John 15:1-2 TPT

Let's revisit Genesis 1:28 NLT: ***"Then God blessed them and said, "Be fruitful and multiply. Fill the earth and govern it. Reign over the fish in the sea, the birds in the sky, and all the animals that scurry along the ground."***

The first point we made was **"Be Fruitful."** The second point I want to make is, **"Multiply"** and the third point is, **"Replenish the earth."**

Funny enough, most of us have no problem with point number three, replenishing the earth. Probably the misconception is that we think number three is the only application to the scripture. This is not only about having babies, fruitfulness and multiplication apply to every facet of life. The word **"Multiply"** in this context means to increase in every regard, in whatever area and part of who you are. God is expecting increase. **Increase in whatever respect to bring in abundance, to be great, to grow up and to be exceedingly and excessively capable and able.** Considering what God has put in you that's not too much to ask for! Don't you agree?

THE KEY OF GENEROSITY

There is seed in you and the nature of the seed in you is to increase, replicate, multiply. Take the little that you have and convert it into great exceeding abundance not just in one area but in *every* area. God promises to bless whatever you put your hand to. The key to unlocking this particular blessing is generosity.

> ***"Give generously to them and do so without a grudging heart; then because of this the Lord your God will bless you in all your work and in everything you put your hand to."*** Deuteronomy 15:10 NIV.

With promises like this it's virtually impossible to fail. Maybe this is the secret Jews have for success. They understand and believe God's promises.

What areas of life is God expecting to bless you? Whichever one you put your hand to. I don't think you understood that! Which areas is God expecting to bless in your life? Whichever one you lay your hand on.

PRODUCTIVITY

This brings us to the second key: ***"Sow your seed in the morning, and at evening let your hands not be idle, for you do not know which will succeed, whether this or that, or whether both will do equally well."*** Ecclesiastes 11:6 NIV

"Whatever your hand finds to do, do it with all your might, for in the realm of the dead, where you are going, there is neither working nor planning nor knowledge nor wisdom.

Do not confuse striving with this doing. Striving is failing to find your rest in him and pushing things in your own strength." Ecclesiastes 9:10 NIV

This means get off that couch, turn off the television, quit fiddling on your phone and do something! Productiveness is a vehicle for blessing and prosperity. You just can't name it and claim it; you must put your hand to work too! This is about valuing the person God made you to be and treasuring what he has put in you. **Respond in faith to what God has already put in you by continuing to enlarge and excel.**

People who have understood this concept have developed incredible resources and financial empires. **There is a dynasty in each one of us screaming to manifest.** Every empire and dynasty begun as a little seed, put the seed in you to work and see what happens.

How far do you continue to exceed and excel? What are the limits, what are the boundaries? The word is present continuous. If you made 70 billion-dollars should you stop there? If you did you would be a poor steward. How do we feel about the rich getting richer? How much money can anybody possibly have? The question is not about the amount of money a person has, it's the heart attitude towards the money and understanding why God has blessed you. I think I have said enough about this. **God blesses us to be a blessing.** The more money we have the more people we can bless. If you understand that all the riches and wealth you can ever have is God's, you won't have a problem.

Let me show you the picture or the illustration of Genesis 26:13. He talks about Isaac; he says the man became rich and his wealth continued to grow until he became very wealthy. Does that make sense to you? What is the nature of wealth? It grows. **What has God placed within you?** The seed for wealth, the seed for increase and multiplication.

It is your natural state of existence to continue to grow until you become exceedingly wealthy. I will leave you with some scriptures.

Psalm 25:13 NIV ***"He will spend his days in prosperity and his descendants will inherit the land."***

You were meant to spend all your days in prosperity.

> Psalm 112:3 NIV ***"Wealth and riches are in his house and his righteousness endures forever."***
>
> Proverbs 8:18 TPT: ***"Unending wealth and glory come to those who discover where I dwell. The riches of righteousness and a long, satisfying life will be given to them."***
>
> Proverbs 10:22 NIV: ***"The blessing of the Lord brings wealth and he adds no sorrow."***

The limitation is our imagination, our lack of understanding. Why I am saying this? To bring understanding and break off the limitation so you can be free to imagine above and beyond so you can come into the above and beyond that God promises you.

What we know today does not matter, what matters most is what we do with what we have. Learning to be the best we can be and being efficient in who we are. That is what is going to bear fruit. That is what is going to make a bigger difference.

Chapter Seven

NEVER EAT YOUR SEED

I WANT to address this issue because it's part of the reason most people don't get ahead. We read in 2 Corinthians 9:10 TPT that God gives the seed to the sower.

> ***"This generous God who supplies abundant seed for the farmer, which becomes bread for our meals, is even more extravagant toward you. First, he supplies every need, plus more. Then he multiplies the seed as you sow it, so that the harvest of your generosity will grow.***

> ***You will be abundantly enriched in every way as you give generously on every occasion, for when we take your gifts to those in need, it causes many to give thanks to God."***

God supplies the seed for one reason and one reason only, so that you can sow the seed. He wants you to have an abundant harvest so you can be generous in your giving to people in need. **When you give to the poor God is glorified.** The scripture paints a picture that seed becomes bread for your meals. This means that when you fail to plant your seed for whatever reason you won't have bread for food.

This reminds me of a period of famine caused by drought in Zambia, Africa in the late 1990s and early 2000s. Southern Africa was experiencing massive food shortages more especially the staples such as corn. As the drought came to a breaking point, aid organizations began pouring resources to bring food security. They provided grants to farmers in villages in terms of corn seed. The idea was for people to sow the corn seed. Following the harvest, the farmers could have plenty of food for their families and sell the surplus for cash to repay the revolving fund.

BREAKING THE CYCLE

This was a great idea to defeat hunger and starvation until the aid recipients begun to wash off the chemicals coated on the corn seed for preservation. They cooked the corn seed and ate the seed. When the harvest season came, they were worse off than before. Now they owe the aid revolving fund and are still hungry. I saw the cycle of poverty continue. Always behind and never getting ahead.

I learnt something through this event. **When you eat your seed, you eat your future and the future of your children.**

The concept of Seed, Time and Harvest guarantees provision of resources for now and the future. When we break this cycle, we sink into lack and poverty. **Poverty is when people eat their seed in order to get through today while debt is living at the expense of the future.**

When we are in debt, we are committing our future resources to our creditors. This means that your future earnings do not belong to you and your children but to your creditors and their children.

This creates a culture of dependence rather than empowerment. Does this mean people should never borrow or get into debt? Well, that depends on why you are borrowing. There is what I would like to think of as "Good debt and Bad debt." Bad debt is what most of us have. This is when we borrow money to buy consumer items. For example, using your credit card to buy things that will never give you a return. What you are actually doing is saying that you are going to take whatever you earn in the future and pay off your debt. The problem with this is that when the future comes you will be broke so you will have to borrow again and again and so continues the cycle of debt.

Good debt is when we borrow seed to plant. I am talking about investment debt, money that makes a return. As opposed to committing our future resources and earning to the creditor. We are only committing a portion of our future harvest of the seed we borrowed.

It always amazes me just how much money people with little means spend on the latest gadgets. Things they can do without. People spend every bit of money they have just to see their Pop Idol at a concert. Stop sacrificing your future, don't eat your seed! Plant for the future. If we are going to break systematic poverty and debt, we need to change our spending habits. **We must prioritize seed sowing over consumerism.**

There is a hard lesson in the Bible from Esau. The man who sold his birthright to his brother because he was hungry. It may have seemed as a good idea at the time. Meeting his present need was more eminent than a firstborn inheritance in the distant future. Esau ate that plate of food he purchased from his brother Jacob without any regard for the future consequences. Esau lost his birthright, a double portion of inheritance just because he was too impatient to wait for mummy to cook! **Don't be like Esau, be patient and plant the seed God has given you.** In due time you will reap an abundant harvest.

"One day when Jacob was cooking some stew, Esau arrived home from the wilderness exhausted and hungry. Esau said to Jacob, "I'm starved! Give me some of that red stew!" (This is how Esau got his other name, Edom, which means "red.") "All right," Jacob replied, "but trade me your rights as the firstborn son." "Look, I'm dying of starvation!" said Esau. "What good is my birthright to me now?"

But Jacob said, "First you must swear that your birthright is mine." So, Esau swore an oath, thereby selling all his rights as the firstborn to his brother, Jacob. Then Jacob gave Esau some bread and lentil stew. Esau ate the meal, then got up and left. He showed contempt for his rights as the firstborn." Genesis 25:29-34 NLT

Giving to people in need

Giving to the needy is an inescapable virtue through the scriptures. We all need to do what we can to break the cycle of poverty without perpetuating dependence. I look at giving to the needy as twofold: one, meet the immediate need;

two, create a platform which empowers people to take control of their own future. Lenders don't want this because they want to keep people enslaved. Give people bread to eat today and seed to plant for tomorrow's provision. **But to achieve this, we need a cultural shift and a change in our mental attitudes.**

I was speaking to a group of students in Myanmar a few years ago. The classes were conducted in a makeshift classroom made of anything they could hammer together. I offered the students a $100 challenge in the local currency. I asked the students to offer suggestions on how they could spend the money if I gave that $100 to them. With great excitement they gave a lot of different ideas. I noticed that all the ideas had one thing in common. It had to do with buying some kind of food to eat.

I challenged the students to think of that $100 as a seed they could plant. I asked the students to think of something they could buy and resell on the street for a profit. They could buy a few cases of bottled water from the local wholesale outlet, cool the water using the refrigerator they had available and sell bottled cold water to tourists.

I offered that I would match them dollar for dollar on whatever profit they made. A few years on, I am still waiting! We have done a similar thing with pastors in Africa on a slightly bigger scale. Those who planted the seed are doing very well but those who ate the seed are still asking for help.

People have been raised to think just for now. If we never learn to save and plant the seed, we are crippling ourselves. We want to be empowering and not enabling. Like I said previously, in every dollar you ever had there was seed in it. There was seed to grow a money tree. A money tree is residual income that keeps on coming and bearing fruit. **This is the secret to wealth creation, invest don't spend!**

As a missionary in Africa, I learnt to ask for seed instead of asking for bread. If you are going to ask your bank for money, you might as well ask for seed money. I can hear some of you saying, "What if the investment doesn't work out?" Well, if you took out a loan to go on a holiday you will still be in debt anyway! I would rather take a chance on something with a prospect of a return.

I will talk a bit more about this subject in the next Chapter **"Dealing with the Fear of Failure."**

When I was about twelve years old my mom left me with my then alcoholic father. She had had enough of the domestic violence and need a break. She left me with about $50 for groceries and food, not knowing for how long she would be gone or if she was ever coming back. Faced with this uncertain prospect I knew that if I ran out of money I would possibly starve. I thought of the $50 as a seed. I walked for 15km/9.32 miles on very unfriendly paths for a twelve-year-old child alone. I went to the wholesale store and bought five packets of cigarettes. When I returned home, I sold the cigarettes by the stick to the airmen at the junior officers club. When the cigarettes sold out, I walked again this time I bought ten packets. I repeated this process until I could afford to pay for public transport and buy cartons of cigarette packs.

When my mom returned home after a month of being away, I handed her about $150. I gave her back the $50 she gave me plus $100 return. I clearly remember those tears of joy on my mother's face.

She didn't know what she was coming back home to or what we were going to live on. Her little boy planted the seed to save the day. **From that moment I become a sower.** I diversified my business from selling sticks of cigarettes to gardening. I used some of my proceeds to buy tomato, onion and cabbage seeds. I recruited a friend to work with me on my gardening project. This was a great success financially for two twelve-year-olds. I further diversified into payday loans. This is where I learnt percentages. Looking back, I can't believe that I had service men getting loans from a twelve-year-old!

As a boy I never asked my parents for pocket money, clothes or toys. I had enough to buy my own and help out. It doesn't take much to make something of ourselves if we are willing to take a chance. In whatever I receive, I recognize that there is seed. In your pay-check there is seed. In that $50 birthday or Christmas present from Aunty Ruth there is seed. **I treat any unexpected money or income I receive as seed.** Unexpected income is not for spending, it's for sowing.

Don't spend your bonuses or overtime pay, treat it as seed money find some good soil to plant it in. In due season you will have a great harvest.

Don't live today at the expense of the future, don't live for the moment, invest for the future. Don't be pressured to keep up with the trends, take control of your financial future. My kids would say, can we have the Xbox because some of their friends got one. I would say to my kids; you can buy the game console or invest money to secure your financial future. What do you choose? The simple choices and decisions you make today will greatly impact how your tomorrow turns out. Whenever possible plant the seed.

Our world view is back to front, we see seed in the fruit instead of fruit in the seed. I find it interesting that we have even genetically engineered seedless fruit. Somehow seed in the fruit is considered as an inconvenience. Without seed there is no perpetuity of productivity and fruitfulness. Every seed has fruit inside it just like every fruit has seed. This speaks of ongoing reproduction and multiplication. The problem with a handout is that it is fruit without seed.

Years ago, a western aid organization offered seed for Genetically Modified Corn to starving African countries. GMO, they called it. It was a good gesture of good will. But the problem was when the GMO corn cross pollinated with the regular crop planted by the poor farmers, they could not re-use the corn seed like they had done for many years. The grain from the GMO corn could not reproduce or the famers would be required to obtain special permission. In the meantime, the local corn is extinct.

SUMMARY

- GOD HAS GIVEN US EVERYTHING WE NEED BOTH FOR LIFE AND GODLINESS

  For everything we will ever need God has deposited the **SEED** necessary for us to develop into a people we were born to be.

- **YOUR DESTINY IS the SEED OF GOD'S PURPOSE FOR YOU.**

  If you create the necessary conditions, your seed will become a mighty OAK.

- WHY WOULD GOD CHOOSE TO GIVE YOU A SEED OVER PROVISION?

  Because HIS desire is for you to increase and multiply in every sense.

- SEED is God's blessing within you that keeps on producing for you and future generations, WHILE PROVISION only has one life CYCLE.

  God doesn't just want to provide for you, HIS desire is for the seed in you to increase and make provision for generations yet to come.

  God's blessings come in seed form because He wants to prosper you.

  God can give you bread, and you will live for a day. He can give a grain of wheat and you can live for a lifetime.

- FISH OR FISHING LESSONS?

  I vote fishing lessons any day.

- GOD's design of multiplication IS THROUGH SEED. THE INHERENT QUALITY OF EVERY SEED IS NOT TO REMAIN ALONE.

  In the right atmosphere the seed is destined to increase.

  GOD sows the seed in your life, prophetic words, promises, etc. He sows hope, life and blessings.

- YOUR HEART IS A GREENHOUSE.

  Create an environment that would maximize the potential of your seed.

  Surround yourself with like-minded people. People who want what you want. People who encourage, educate and fight for your success rather than stand in the way.

- THE ENEMY IS AFTER YOUR SEED

  John10:10 TPT ***"A thief has only one thing in mind– he wants to steal, slaughter, and destroy.***

But I have come to give you everything in abundance, more than you expect –life in its fullness until you overflow!"

The enemy wants to kill, steal and destroy. His goal is to terrorize and cause fear in your life. **Fear is like ACID IN THE SOIL. It kills all potential seed you sow.** Fear conditions your heart for a crop failure. **Fear ABORT's THE DREAM in your life.**

- WHICH SEED ARE YOU TENDING? What is your heart incubating? GOD's seed or the enemy's seed of Doubt?

Chapter Eight

Dealing With the Fear of Failure

FAILURE is one of life's consistent occurrences. We all have dealt with failure at one point or another. **Failures should never define us, it's how we handle failure that defines us.** Failure is not indicative of your capacity, ability or potential, it only demonstrates a process that does not work. I look at failure as a path to discovery. It's a process which allows for review, fine tuning and perfection. Mistakes and failure are necessary for your success. They are part of the journey to greatness; hence we cannot allow ourselves to live in the shadows of the fear of making mistakes and failing. People who have never failed at anything are people who failed to try anything.

We were all born to leave a legacy. None of us are meant to die like we never existed. Imprint your mark for the next generation to know that once upon a time you were here! You were not meant to exist in obscurity and quietly slip away into the afterlife. Success and failure are about ideas, processes and outcomes. It's usually not about people, so you should not take failure too personal. Your value and worth are not in what you do but in who you were created to be. People may not like your idea, process of doing things or the outcome of your undertaking but they can still love you. They will respect you for having tried. Show me a full life lived and I will show you a thousand mistakes and epic fails.

We only fail when we stop trying! The Bible says that, ***"For the lovers of God may suffer adversity and stumble seven times, but they will continue to rise over and over again. But the unrighteous are brought down by just one calamity and will never be able to rise again."*** Proverbs 24:16 TPT

QUALIFIED BY DISQUALIFICATION

What makes the Bible relevant to us is the humanity and the failures of our heroes. We are inspired and encouraged by the demonstrative grace and the love of God in moments of failure and weakness. Time and time again throughout scripture we see epic failures become stories of epic redemption. I am convinced that if you have experienced some setbacks, God is rewriting your story. He will do what He does best, turning tragic moments into great testimonies. **Never allow failure to disqualify you.** I tend to think of myself as qualified by my disqualification.

"But God chose those whom the world considers foolish to shame those who think they are wise, and God chose the puny and powerless to shame the high and mighty. He chose the lowly, the laughable in the world's eyes–nobodies–so that he would shame the somebodies.

For he chose what is regarded as insignificant in order to supersede what is regarded as prominent, so that there would be no place for prideful boasting in God's presence.

For it is not from man that we draw our life but from God as we are being joined to Jesus, the Anointed One. And now he is our God-given wisdom, our virtue, our holiness, and our redemption." 1 Corinthians 1:27-30 TPT

We could look at Abraham and Isaac who lied about their wives. Jacob the trickster, Judah who slept with his daughter in law. Rahab the prostitute who happens to be in the family tree of our Lord Jesus. David who committed adultery and murdered the woman's husband. The list goes on to Peter who denied Jesus three times. Paul who murdered Christians! Somehow none of these people are remembered for their mistakes and failures. We honor and celebrate them for their ability and resilience to rise from the ruins of shame, failure and despair. **It is their courage to try again and again that has immortalized them as heroes in the halls of faith.**

This is one of my personal favorites, ***"But God removed Saul and replaced him with David, a man about whom God said, 'I have found David son of Jesse, a man after my own heart. He will do everything I want him to do."*** Acts 13:22 NLT

How does one move up from wife-stealing and husband-murdering to be a man after God's own heart? David learnt something King Saul never did. ***The key to success is learning from your mistakes.*** Don't dwell on your mistakes, repent, ask for forgiveness and move on! Leave the past where it belongs, behind you! David also purposed and positioned himself to pursue God's heart and to accomplish all that God destined for him to do. This is paramount, there is grace for you to do what God has destined for you to do. **Where there is grace, there is favor.** Favor will lead you through a path of least resistance.

DEALING WITH THE FEAR OF FAILURE

Be adaptable, don't be set in your ways like concrete. Be like water, flow and adapt to your conditions and environment. Humility and teachability is an integral part of success. Proverbs 3:5-6 TPT says this, ***"Trust in the Lord completely, and do not rely on your own opinions. With all your heart rely on him to guide you, and he will lead you in every decision you make.***

Become intimate with him in whatever you do, and he will lead you wherever you go. Don't think for a moment that you know it all."

If you are visionary, most people will not fully understand or comprehend the ideas you bring to the table. This means that more often than not your ideas and proposals will be rejected. **Sometimes you need to allow time for people to catch up to your brilliance.** When electricity was introduced for use in the homes in England it took 50 years for the general public to embrace the idea. For 50 years it must have felt like an epic failure and I am sure the investors lost hope on ever getting a return.

British scientist William Sturgeon invented the first commutator DC electric motor capable of turning machinery in 1832. Yet more than 100 years later on the world was still using steam engines. We are still driving around in fossil fuel vehicles. Sometimes habits die hard. Many times, there is a very thin line between genius and failure. **Most failures are great ideas at the wrong time and wrong place.** The same can be said about success. It's a great idea at the right time and the right place.

My family enjoyed Kentucky Fried Chicken (KFC) and Krispy Kreme donuts. A couple of times a week we would drive to the next suburb to buy some as we didn't have these establishments locally. I would say to myself that if anyone ever set up shop in my neighborhood, they would make a lot of money. Truth be told, I did apply to get the franchise rights for KFC, unfortunately someone beat me to it. At about the same time both KFC and Krispy Kreme came to town, you wouldn't believe this, the week before they opened shop, my whole family collectively decided to go on a gluten free, low carb and no sugar lifestyle.

I find that more and more people are adopting healthy habits and lifestyle. This makes me wonder, what if Colonel Sanders the successful founder of the KFC franchise was to start KFC today? It would probably be a failure. It was a great idea at the time but would not be met with the similar level of success in today's market.

Failure allows us to evaluate our position and strategy. It gives us an opportunity to change what does not work and make improvements on what works. It is said of Thomas Edison that he never failed 1000 times on the light bulb. He only learnt 1000 ways why it doesn't work.

Fear of failure is just it, it's only fear. I know you may have genuine reasons and concerns. Maybe you tried and feel that you lost big time. But I want you to understand that fear of failure is a train to nowhere. If you are afraid of failing, I assure you that you have already failed. **Fear is the snare the enemy uses to keep you separated from your potential.** Fear is misguided faith and that's what makes it a sin. It means that you have your trust and confidence in the whispers of the accuser than you have in the word and promises of God.

When God is our focus, we become alive to all the possibilities we have in him. His faithfulness is far bigger than our deepest and darkest fears. His love permeates our being and drives out all fear. Never allow fear to drive you away from your dreams and prospects.

"Love never brings fear, for fear is always related to punishment. But love's perfection drives the fear of punishment far from our hearts.

Whoever walks constantly afraid of punishment has not reached love's perfection.

Our love for others is our grateful response to the love God first demonstrated to us." 1 John 4:18-19 TPT

A GOOD PLACE TO START

Repent for placing your faith in the negative rather than the positive and believing the voice of the enemy instead of the voice of God. **Any voice that belittles your capacity and breaks your confidence is not from God.** God's voice is reassuring, affirming and life-giving even in correction. It never makes you feel silly, stupid or condemned. Fear is as distinct from love as day is from night. ***"This is the message we heard from Jesus and now declare to you: God is light, and there is no darkness in him at all."*** 1 John 1:5 NLT. 2 Timothy 1:7 TPT has this advice, ***"For God will never give you the spirit of fear, but the Holy Spirit who gives you mighty power, love, and self-control."***

Better yet, Romans 8:15-16 TPT, ***"And you did not receive the "spirit of religious duty," leading you back into the fear of never being good enough.***

But you have received the "Spirit of full acceptance," enfolding you into the family of God.

And you will never feel orphaned, for as he rises up within us, our spirits join him in saying the words of tender affection, "Beloved Father!"

For the Holy Spirit makes God's fatherhood real to us as he whispers into our innermost being, "You are God's beloved child!"

Some people are too afraid to try so they dig a hole and burry their talents. The Lord told a story to this effect. ***"Again, heaven's kingdom realm is like the wealthy man who went on a long journey and summoned all his trusted servants and assigned his financial management over to them. Before he left on his journey, he entrusted a bag of five thousand gold coins to one of his servants, to another a bag of two thousand gold coins, and to the third a bag of one thousand gold coins, each according to his ability to manage.***

"The one entrusted with five thousand gold coins immediately went out and traded with the money, and he doubled his investment. In the same way, the one who was entrusted with two thousand gold coins traded with the sum and likewise doubled his investment. But the one who had been entrusted with one thousand gold coins dug a hole in the ground and buried his master's money.

"After much time had passed, the master returned to settle accounts with his servants. The one who was entrusted with five thousand gold coins came and brought ten thousand, saying, 'See, I have doubled your money.' "Commending his servant, the master replied, 'You have done well, and proven yourself to be my loyal and trustworthy servant. Because you have been a faithful steward to manage a small sum, now I will put you in charge of much, much more. You will experience the delight of your master, who will say to you, "Come celebrate with me!"

"Then the one who had been entrusted with two thousand gold coins came in and said, 'See, my master, I have doubled what you have entrusted

to me.' "Commending his servant, the master replied, 'You have done well, and proven yourself to be my loyal and trustworthy servant. Because you were faithful to manage a small sum, now I will put you in charge of much, much more. You will experience the delight of your master, who will say to you, "Come celebrate with me!"

"Then the one who had been entrusted with one thousand gold coins came to his master and said, 'Look, sir. I know that you are a hard man to please and you're a shrewd and ruthless businessman who grows rich on the backs of others. I was afraid of you, so I went and hid your money and buried it in the ground. But here it is–take it, it's yours.'

"Angered by what he heard, the master said to him, 'You're an untrustworthy and lazy servant! If you knew I was a shrewd and ruthless businessman who always makes a profit, why didn't you deposit my money in the bank? Then I would have received it all back with interest when I returned. But because you were unfaithful, I will take the one thousand gold

coins and give them to the one who has ten thousand. For the one who has will be given more, until he overflows with abundance. And the one with hardly anything, even what little he has will be taken from him.'

"Then the master said to his other servants, 'Now, throw that good-for-nothing servant far away from me into the outer darkness, where there will be great misery and anguish!" Matthew 24:14-30 TPT

WHEN THINGS DON'T GO ACCORDING TO PLAN

When things don't go according to plan, evaluate, regroup make necessary changes and try again! Which one of the three gentlemen in the parable above would you say you are? **Learn to look at failure as not the end but a beginning of a new path to a great adventure.** Every successful story is built on the foundation of failure.

The only difference is that some people gave up along the way while others pushed on past their breaking point.

Failure also reveals our limitations. This is a good opportunity to seek help and advice. ***"Your plans will fall apart right in front of you if you fail to get good advice. But if you first seek out multiple counselors, you'll watch your plans succeed."*** Proverbs 15:22 TPT

> ***"Without wise leadership, a nation falls; there is safety in having many advisers."*** Proverbs 11:14 NLT
>
> ***"Listen well to wise counsel and be willing to learn from correction so that by the end of your life you'll be known for your wisdom."*** Proverbs 19:20 TPT
>
> ***"Wise strategy is necessary to wage war, and with many astute advisers you'll see the path to victory more clearly."*** Proverbs 24:6 TPT

The short end of the point I am making is Proverbs 12:15 TPT, ***"A fool is in love with his own opinion, but wisdom means being teachable."***

Chapter Nine

CREATING A CULTURE OF CELEBRATION

IF you are to be successful, you will have to develop a culture of celebration. **Learn to celebrate your own achievements as well as the successes of other people.** Celebration is pertinent to gratitude and thanksgiving. It helps us recognize God's hand and grace on our lives and others. This will enhance your ability to partner with the Holy Spirit, His work in your life and those around you. **In the absence of a culture of celebration we become cynical, critical and judgmental.**

You must understand that when you are cynical, it's not just the person you are criticizing and judging. You are criticizing the Holy Spirit and the grace of God at work in that person. You go to war with God by cursing His work.

God's promise to Abraham was, ***"I will bless those who bless you and curse those who treat you with contempt. All the families on earth will be blessed through you."*** Genesis 12:3 NLT. Acknowledging and celebrating God's blessing on someone else unlocks blessings and favor in your own life. The Pharisees blasphemed against God by attributing the works of Jesus to the devil. "***But some of them said, "No wonder he can cast out demons. He gets his power from Satan, the prince of demons."*** Luke 11:15 NLT. When we fail to bless and celebrate the grace of God in others, we become obstructionist instead of a channel of blessings.

THE PRINCIPLE OF BLESSING

This reality is more emphasized when it comes to financial blessings and prosperity.

If we cannot celebrate other people's prosperity, we open ourselves up to a spirit of envy and jealousy. Remember the principle of blessing in Genesis 12:3? The same applies here! Bless and celebrate successful people and you will unlock success. If you can't celebrate success you will fight against success. If you can't celebrate prosperity you will fight against prosperity. **You can never breakthrough in areas you fail to honor.**

Prosperity and financial breakthrough are often tied or connected to the prosperity and breakthrough of people around you. The Lord taught me this principle when I left Africa and moved to Australia. I am one of those Africans who are proud of being African. I had a great desire to serve and contribute to the wellbeing and development of Africa. Yes! I did have an ambition and a plan to one day become President of Zambia. So, moving to Australia felt like abandoning the very people I was trying to serve. I felt like I was being part of the massive drain of human resources out of Africa.

While wrestling with this whole thought God spoke to me through Jeremiah 29:7 NIV ***"Also, seek the peace and prosperity of the city to which I have***

carried you into exile. Pray to the Lord for it, because if it prospers, you too will prosper." There it was! Like most of us, I knew Jeremiah 29:11 but never paid attention to verse 7. ***"For I know the plans I have for you," declares the Lord, "plans to prosper you and not to harm you, plans to give you hope and a future."***

I knew God had a plan to prosper me, but I never understood that His plan for my prosperity is intertwined with the prosperity of people and places He sends me to. **God invites us to seek and work for the prosperity of the people around us.** He calls us to pray for their blessing. Every Pastor knows this! When people in your congregation are poor so are you. When your congregation is wealthy and prosperous so are you. God blesses you as you bless others. Blessing others is saying "AMEN" to what God is doing. This helps to align your heart to God's heart. You become a partner with God in fighting for the wellbeing of His people instead of fighting against God.

The act of blessing other people is a weapon of warfare. It counters the narcissistic spirit at work even among Christians. It brings down jealousy, envy, criticism, cynicism, judgmental attitudes and competition. God never intended for you to compete with anybody. The only person you should ever compete against is yourself. **Don't compete, be a completer!** Growth means beating your personal best and record not another person's record. What good would it do if you beat Usain Bolt's 100m record if God has called you to run cross-country? Bless and celebrate people for who they are. Applaud their achievements and success and you will be better for it.

BLESSING THE RICH AND WEALTHY

Yes, I know...! I remember this feeling as a poor African attending a prayer rally with Lou Engle in Australia. He called on us prayer warriors to pray for Australia and the United States of America.

For some reason I felt offended by this idea of asking me to pray for these rich people who have never known a day of starvation in their entire lives. Back home in Africa people were sleeping on the floor in hospitals because there are too many sick people and very little resources. My list went on and on to justify why I could not spend time praying for the "Rich People." Actually, I left the prayer rally to have a little one-on-one discussion with God about the matter. It seemed to me like God favored the rich over the poor. I gave God an opportunity to explain Himself and He did!

God was very thorough and extensive in His response to my challenge. I talk about this when I share about generational curses and blessings. The summary of this interlude with Abba is Jeremiah 29:7. ***"Also, seek the peace and prosperity of the city to which I have carried you into exile. Pray to the Lord for it, because if it prospers, you too will prosper."*** NIV

What I am saying is that there is a certain sense of agitation most people experience when it comes to the rich and wealthy. The general feeling is that rich people exploit the poor. This makes it really hard to celebrate the rich if you are coming from this school of thought. However, this also places a cap on your ability to break through from lack to a place of abundance. **You curse yourself by cursing others and bless yourself by blessing others.**

MY WORST FLIGHT

I felt most challenged and confronted by the disparities between the rich and the poor on airplane flights. If you ever fly coach or economy like most of us, you notice the difference between the classes: First, Business and Economy. The worst thing is when you board the plane from the front doors you walk through the business class. It's evident that things are very different in business-class. First-class is a different planet altogether! I would walk through business-class and see how the others live and fly. Those nice extendible comfortable seats, priority service and so on.

I would enviously walk through business-class cursing under my breath about the stupid rich people. Then I would start talking to myself, "What kind of an idiot would spend 4 to 10 times the fare so they could fly business or first class?" Why can't they save the money by flying economy like the rest of us and use the money to help the poor. More especially those pastors and evangelists, they ought to be ashamed of themselves. Yes…! I was judging everybody on business-class. Clearly, I was harboring resentment issues in my heart, it just feels so unfair and unjustifiable that some people can live in such obscene luxury while the rest of us are stiff and sore. I was self-righteous like the disciples who got offended with Jesus, when Mary Magdalene "wasted" that jar of costly perfume.

"While he was eating, a woman came in with a beautiful alabaster jar of expensive perfume and poured it over his head. The disciples were indignant when they saw this. "What a waste!" they said. "It could have been sold for a high price and the money given to the poor." Matthew 26:7-8 NLT

I failed to bless and celebrate the business-class passengers until one day I was on a 14-hour flight. Just after take-off one of the passengers got airsick and vomited on me big-time. Not just a little vomit, I mean a big-time vomit! I am on a plane; my clothes are in check-in luggage. I have vomit on me! The flight attendant took one look at me and disappeared. She soon returned with some replacements she had found ~ some pajamas from Business-Class. My first thought was, *"Why don't you upgrade me to Business-Class so that I don't have to smell vomit in this seat for the next 14 hours?"* God's response was, ***"No! You can't go to Business-Class because you are mad and offended with everyone up there."***

I could not have what I have been cursing. On that flight I repented for every unkind word I had ever said about people in Business-Class. Every time I walk through Business-Class to my economy seat, I bless those wonderful people who definitely have earned it and deserve to be there. I would say, "Father thank you for these Business-Class people, whatever they did to be in these seats, do it for me." Then something strange began to happen to me. I would get pulled out of the queue and get upgraded to Business-Class. My wife also started getting upgraded. My life is an upgrade. **As I bless others, I unlock the same blessing for myself and my family.**

The moment you become resentful and begin to curse someone's position or status you cut yourself off from ever attaining that position and status. You turn off a switch connecting you to that blessing, that position can never become your goal. Your inspiration is limited by your desire. You can't pursue something or ever want to achieve or aspire to or live up to something you are offended with. **The principle that you must learn and develop is a culture of blessing the things you want the most in life.**

This totally changed my attitude towards people who are living their dream life. **I can celebrate their success and achievement without the need to compete or cut them down to size.** I am creating an environment where tall poppies can grow and flourish. The tall-poppy syndrome gets you nowhere, it's a dis-service to humanity. It's anti-blessing, don't do it! Until you change your attitude and your mindset nothing will ever change. It's difficult to have financial breakthrough if you are angry with everyone who has got a breakthrough. Why? Because you can't learn from any breakthrough ideas and processes that brought them success. **Never allow your attitude to stand in the way of progress both for you and others.**

When God decided to upgrade me to business-class, I found myself in the position I had always resented. Do you think I was upset being in there? No, actually I was like, *"This is cool! Father, can we do this all the time?"* I now appreciated the slickness of those lounge seats in there. Before my upgrade experience I never ever thought of asking God for an upgrade to Business-Class because I was angry with it and everybody in it. These days every time I am anywhere near a plane guess what discussion I am having with My Father. Since I began to embrace Business-Class travel, I have been upgraded several times. Every time I fly I expect to be upgraded. This doesn't always happen, but it never hurts to try.

The worst thing you can ever do is resent the Joneses, learn from the Joneses, bless the Joneses. The Joneses have been on journey to get to where they are. There is a lot you can learn when you are open-minded. God can use anybody and anything to speak and teach you something. He used a donkey to speak to Balaam, why not the Joneses? It's much easier to see the way forward when we are not navel-gazing. We become tunnel-visioned and lose focus of the big picture. Small mindedness has never done anyone any good.

Want for others what you want for yourself. **Bless other people with the same blessing you would like for your family.** This is the Golden Rule!

Jesus said it like this, ***"In everything you do, be careful to treat others in the same way you'd want them to treat you, for that is the essence of all the teachings of the Law and the Prophets."*** Matthew 7:12 TPT

In my teen years I was asked to preach at a youth overnight prayer gathering. There were two other, older, mature and more seasoned preachers scheduled to speak before me. I was asked to take the graveyard session, that's about 3am when everyone is falling asleep. This shift is usually reserved for the most anointed and dynamic preachers who preach up a storm and keep everyone hooked to every word at 3am in the morning. I didn't think I was that preacher. So, I fasted and spent every minute I could praying for myself for God to anoint me.

Somewhere in there God interrupted my prayer meeting. He said, ***"Son, I don't want you to spend any time at all praying for yourself and your session, I want you to spend all your time praying for the other two speakers!"*** That's unfair, the other two guys will be highly anointed and look better than me I thought to myself.

But what do you do when God gives such a direct and clear word? So, I obeyed and prayed for my brothers with every fibre in my being. I never spared a moment to utter a quick prayer for myself. Before long it was my time to speak. Boy was I anointed! Everybody was on their toes and the Holy Spirit hit the place like a hurricane. I learnt something that day. **By heaping blessing on others, I was actually heaping the same blessing on myself and ministry.** Whenever I find myself in a similar situation, I focus on praying and blessing others.

> ***"Speak blessing, not cursing, over those who reject and persecute you. Celebrate with those who celebrate, and weep with those who grieve.***
>
> ***Live happily together in a spirit of harmony and be as mindful of another's worth as you are your own.***
>
> ***Don't live with a lofty mind-set, thinking you are too important to serve others, but be willing to do menial tasks and identify with those who are humble minded.***

Don't be smug or even think for a moment that you know it all.

Never hold a grudge or try to get even but plan your life around the noblest way to benefit others.

Do your best to live as everybody's friend." Romans 12:14-17 TPT

"When someone curses you, bless that person in return. When you are mistreated and harassed by others, accept it as your mission to pray for them." Luke 6:28 TPT

Chapter Ten
Be Adaptable

YOU probably have heard the saying, "You can't teach an old dog a new trick." While I acknowledge that as we get older, we become set in our ways of doing things, adapting to change in this fast-paced world gets increasingly difficult and challenging. But if we are to remain relevant to the times we live in and thrive in the present current market economy, we will need to be very adaptable. Adaptability doesn't mean abandoning your core values, but finding the most effective way to be the best you can be and maximize your performance in any given environment.

Your core values are an anchor point for stability and a mural of who you are. **Never sacrifice who you are for the sake of fitting in.** God never intended for you fit in but to fit out so can make a difference.

Don't be the proverbial old dog. Make learning a lifestyle. **The moment you stop learning you cease to develop and grow.** Keep an open mind to new possibilities. The future belongs to those who embrace change. Change is inevitable, you might as well make it your ally. The rule to modern survival is adapt or die! This could mean constantly keeping your skills up to date with current industry trends and requirements. Otherwise you will be replaced or lose your market share to more adaptable operators. Whatever skills you don't use you will lose. I am a PC-Tech trained as a client support technician. I have not used a PC since Windows XP. Whenever I am presented with a new Windows computer I am at a loss, I have absolutely no idea what to do with it. This means I am unemployable as a PC-Tech.

Some years back I met a field electrician. He worked for a big energy company fixing electrical faults in the field. It was his last week on the job because the company was introducing a new policy. Until now, this highly skilled electrician would go out in the field to do his job. He would write a report of what he had done on a form. He would then hand in his report form at the office for someone else to enter the report in the computer. The new policy his company introduced required every electrician to enter his own report in the computer back at the office. The company offered training to enable this gentleman and his colleagues to keep up with their work requirements. Some people took the opportunity and thrived, but most of the older electricians left the company because they were unwilling to learn a new skill.

CONFRONT YOUR WORST FEARS

Adaptability may mean confronting your worst fears. It could be the scariest thing you can ever do, but you can never overcome what you avoid confronting. There is no victory without a battle. **There are no heroes without giants to be conquered.** Look at change as an opportunity for expansion. Most of us have been raised with the attitude of, "If it's not broken, don't fix it." But it sure can do with some improvements and upgrades. Nobody still watches their old black and white television though it still works perfectly. **By resisting change and failing to adapt we forfeit our share in the future.**

Keep up with the times and seasons, don't let traditions keep you from your destiny. Traditions are a vital container for preserving our culture and history. They are a marker of where we have been and, in some way, a good predictor of where we are likely to end up. This means that in order to plot a different trajectory of the future we may have to dispense with certain traditions otherwise we are bound to replicate the past results and outcome. If you want to see a change, you can't keep on doing what you have always done.

God says, ***"See, I am doing a new thing! Now it springs up; do you not perceive it? I am making a way in the wilderness and streams in the wasteland."*** Isaiah 43:19 NIV.

THE POWER OF PERSPECTIVE

This is a powerful statement which requires a paradigm shift. Unless there is a fundamental change in our general perception and attitude, we are more likely to approach the new thing God is doing with our same old underlying assumptions. For you to have any shares of stock in this new thing God is doing, you must adjust your sight and begin to see things from the new perspective. **Your life will always be in alignment with your point of view.**

One of the most successful tribes in Israel were the sons of Issachar. ***"From the tribe of Issachar, there were 200 leaders of the tribe with their relatives. All these men understood the signs of the times and knew the best course for Israel to take."*** 1 Chronicles 12:32 NLT. These men were very effective because of their ability to adapt to the times and seasons. Whenever they sensed a shift in the nation, they broke tradition and moved with what God was doing. **Be where God is today not where he used to be!**

That is what religion is. Relationship is where God is today. Why? Because relationship is dynamic and constantly evolving. **This requires constant change and forward motion.**

For 40 years God led the Israelites through the wilderness. He led them by a pillar of cloud by day and fire by night. Look at this in Numbers 9:17-23 NLT: ***"Whenever the cloud lifted from over the sacred tent, the people of Israel would break camp and follow it. And wherever the cloud settled, the people of Israel would set up camp. In this way, they traveled and camped at the Lord's command wherever he told them to go. Then they remained in their camp as long as the cloud stayed over the Tabernacle.***

If the cloud remained over the Tabernacle for a long time, the Israelites stayed and performed their duty to the Lord. Sometimes the cloud would stay over the Tabernacle for only a few days, so the people would stay for only a few days, as the Lord commanded.

Then at the Lord's command they would break camp and move on. Sometimes the cloud stayed only overnight and lifted the next morning.

But day or night, when the cloud lifted, the people broke camp and moved on. Whether the cloud stayed above the Tabernacle for two days, a month, or a year, the people of Israel stayed in camp and did not move on.

But as soon as it lifted, they broke camp and moved on. So, they camped or traveled at the Lord's command, and they did whatever the Lord told them through Moses."

Everyone had to keep an eye on that pillar of cloud by day and fire by night and be ready to move at a moment's notice. Those who failed to move when God moved fell behind and were killed by the enemy.

"Never forget what the Amalekites did to you as you came from Egypt. They attacked you when you were exhausted and weary, and they struck down those who were straggling behind. They had no fear of God." Deuteronomy 25:17-18 NLT.

The same is still true today, if you can't adapt and change with the times you are relegating yourself to history instead of the future. It's dying a slow death, you become a relic of the past destined for decommissioning.

Be proactive, utilize every opportunity to set yourself up for the future. Don't let your current success box you in from being better. **The biggest threat to your "GREATNESS" is "GOOD."** As humans, when we get to a good place, we have the propensity to settle. We tend to stop challenging and pushing the boundaries of our limitations. Why settle for good if you can be better? You were born for greatness; okay isn't good enough. "Give me an AMEN!" **It's time to break out of that good box and pursue greatness.**

One of the saddest stories in the Bible is found in I Samuel 16:1 NLT ***"Now the Lord said to Samuel, "You have mourned long enough for Saul. I have rejected him as king of Israel, so fill your flask with olive oil and go to Bethlehem. Find a man named Jesse who lives there, for I have selected one of his sons to be my king."***

God rejected Saul as king over Israel and chose David to replace him. Everybody knew about it and even sung songs about the exploits of David. Yet they continued following Saul as king for over 20 years collectively! Why on earth would anyone do that? It was evident that the spirit of God was on David and Saul was demon oppressed. **Still people could not make the transition from the old to the new because they had it good with Saul.** He provided them with job security, wives, land and so on. They felt they had all they needed under Saul and did not see the urgency or need to align themselves with God's choice and purpose.

Some people would argue that they continued to follow Saul because David was still a young boy. To that I say read 2 Chronicles 24:1-2 NLT. ***"Joash was seven years old when he became king, and he reigned in Jerusalem forty years. His mother was Zibiah from Beersheba. Joash did what was pleasing in the Lord's sight throughout the lifetime of Jehoiada the priest."***

DON'T BE AN OLD DOG

Learn some new tricks, it's never too late to learn something new. This will help your mind stay active and alert. It's a good brain exercise. **A healthy mind is a productive mind.**

Whatever you don't use, you lose. Learn new things this engages your frontal lobe cortex. This part of the brain is involved in motor function, problem solving, spontaneity, memory, language, initiation, judgement, impulse control, and social and sexual behavior. The more this part of your brain stays engaged, the more active it stays. Doing the same routine activities conditions your brain to function in cruise mode. This does not unlock your full potential. **If you have become such a specialist that you can perform your tasks blind folded or in your sleep, then it's time to wake up your brain by learning a new trick.**

Be humble, a know it all attitude will take you nowhere. The secret of human coexistence is interdependence. You have heard it said, *"No man is an Island."* This means that your gifting and abilities are a gift to people around you. And likewise, the people around are also a gift to you. When you are not humble you will struggle to recognize the potential value, other people may add to your life. **The key to humility is having a sober judgment of your own skills, gifting and abilities.** This means that you are neither over selling nor under selling yourself. It's treading that line between who you are and who you are not! Some people over-exaggerate their skills and abilities, when the rubber hits the road they are found lacking. This is called superior pride. Other people impugn their capacity, they rob the world of the gift they are. This is inferior pride.

Be teachable, there is always something new to learn. **Don't ever wear the *"Been there, done that T-shirt".*** The world is on a forward motion. Unteachable people struggle the most to adapt. They tend to reject new ideas. They think their way of doing things is the better way. They lack foresight. We live in a fast-changing world; you must be open to new innovative ideas or risk losing your competitive edge.

This reminds me of the tragic story of Kodak. The year was 1975 when Steve Sasson an engineer at Kodak invented the first Digital Camera. Kodak was a household name. They had a very profitable business selling film for cameras and other consumables associated with photography. They saw the potential of a film-less camera as threat to their lucrative film sales.

Blinded by the success of film sales and other consumables, Kodak failed to see a future without film cameras. The tough lesson to be learnt here is that the world moves on with or without you. This highlights what I said earlier. **The biggest threat to your "GREATNESS" is "GOOD."** Kodak had it so good that even when the digital camera was introduced by other companies, Kodak management didn't notice until their sales began to dwindle. Had Kodak embraced this innovation they would have become leaders in the digital camera market instead playing catch up.

Chapter Eleven

In-Between Seasons

IN most instances people know where they are in life and they also know where they hope to be in future. However, the challenge is how to move on from where they are to where they need or hope to be.

This is the period in life I refer to as the in-between seasons. This season can be one of the most frustrating periods. **Many people are lost in the in-between seasons and never make the transition to the life they hoped to have.**

In this chapter I will give you some pointers on the best way to utilize your time during the in-between seasons. Hopefully this will enable you to convert agitation and frustration of the in-between seasons into positive creative energy to propel you into your future.

INVEST IN YOURSELF

As it is commonly said, **"Today is a gift, tomorrow is a promise."** What you do with your time today matters a lot as it will determine what your tomorrow will become. It is what we *choose* to do with our time today rather than what we feel that shapes our future. Unfortunately, the most misused and wasted time for many people is the in-between seasons. You must understand that, **"Today is training and preparation-day for tomorrow!"** People who fail to prepare for tomorrow are likely to be in the same position as yesterday. You have probably heard it said, **"People don't plan to fail but only fail to plan."**

I am hoping that by now you are getting the idea about *what* you should be doing with your time during the in-between seasons. **Use it for training and preparation for the future.**

Never spend this period in limbo and frustration, make it count by doing something useful. ***I am talking about, diligence, efficiency, stewardship and improving yourself.*** Get your hands dirty. Roll up your sleeves and get to work.

Use the in-between seasons to *invest* in yourself and future. Your future is like a bank account, you can never make a withdrawal out of it if you never made a deposit into it in the first place. If you deposit $1000 into your bank account then you can potentially make a $1000 withdrawal on a future date, more or less depending on the bank fees and interest paid. The illusion a lot of people have is that they want a better, brighter and prosperous future while squandering the opportunities available to them today. ***TODAY IS PREPARATION DAY FOR TOMORROW'S OPPORTUNITIES.***

Make today count because investing is relative, how much time, effort and resources you commit to your future will determine your future reward. Use the in-between seasons to improve yourself, learn something new, read educational books, go to school, seek counsel and advice. Better yet, look for work experiences and volunteer opportunities with people and organizations specializing in areas of your interest.

LEARNING REQUIRES HUMILITY

It takes humility to learn. Have you ever seen those social experiments about how many lost male drivers stop to ask for directions? In a study conducted by a car insurer it was noted that male drivers make an additional 276 miles every year because they are too reluctant to ask for directions. You have to understand that, ***asking for help is not an admission of weakness but courage to confront ignorance and failure.*** Only the brave and most courageous can dare to admit that they need help and reach out to learn from someone else.

Sometimes life and learning can be like dropping your wedding ring in a toilet bowl at a public park. I know, gross! Right? But you are not going to leave your wedding ring in there, no matter how disgusting you will find a way to retrieve it. My point is, **never allow your pride to stand in the way of your progress.** Some people can never progress in life because they are offended with the people they need to learn from. It's like disowning your parents, it doesn't stop them from being your parent, but it can sure stop you from receiving your inheritance. Get over your hang ups! Address any issues which prevent you from benefiting from the skill, wisdom, counsel, experience and resources of the people God has put in your life. Sometimes we just need to eat humble pie. Pride has been the fall of many but has never made a single giant. ***Be willing to put up with minor inconveniences for the sake of the grand prize.***

DEAL WITH YOUR WOUNDING

Some people in this life will never achieve anything or get anywhere of significance because they feel wounded. They are angry with everyone and everything. I have got news for you, *no one owes you anything, you owe it to yourself.* **Deal with your wounding before your wounding deals with you!** It's amazing how many people are stuck in the past because of what someone did or said. You cannot allow anger, pain or bitterness to keep you trapped in the past. Forgive, let go and move on. Don't get through life bleeding on everyone and every opportunity. ***Offence will always build a fence around you barricading you from your opportunities.***

WAIT ON GOD

The in-between seasons is a time to wait on God. Instead of stressing about the future, take time to hear God's heart. The Bible says that, ***"Within your heart you can make plans for your future, but the Lord chooses the steps you take to get there."*** Proverbs 16:9 TPT.

Allow God to *lead* you, after all this life is not your own. It is God who gave it to you, you might as well include Him in your plans. When you take time to wait on God, He renews your strength and gives fresh vision. The prophet Isaiah had this to say: ***"He energizes those who get tired, gives fresh strength to dropouts. For even young people tire and drop out, young folk in their prime stumble and fall. But those who wait upon God get fresh strength.***

They spread their wings and soar like eagles, they run and don't get tired, they walk and don't lag behind." Isaiah 40:29-31 MSG

I usually hear people say they are waiting on God, but in actual fact they are just sitting around waiting for something to happen. This is not what it means to wait on God. Sitting around waiting for something to happen is wishful thinking and time wasting. ***Waiting on God means to rest in God while pursuing revelation and understanding of His plan for you.*** It is to fully engage with God in order to make something happen.

Sometimes while we wait on God, God is waiting on us. Don't delay your destiny by failing to engage with the purpose of God on your life.

LET THE SPIRIT IMPULSES BE YOUR PULSE

"The mature children of God are those who are moved by the impulses of the Holy Spirit." Romans 8:14 TPT.

"Trust God from the bottom of your heart; don't try to figure out everything on your own.

Listen for God's voice in everything you do, everywhere you go; he's the one who will keep you on track.

Don't assume that you know it all. Run to God! Run from evil! Your body will glow with health, your very bones will vibrate with life!" Proverbs 3:5-8 TPT

Remember Psalm 23:1-6? Turn a new leaf and learn from King David. ***"The Lord is my best friend and my shepherd. I always have more than enough. He offers a resting place for me in his luxurious love. His tracks take me to an oasis of peace, the quiet brook of bliss. That's where he restores and revives my life.***

He opens before me pathways to God's pleasure and leads me along in his footsteps of righteousness so that I can bring honor to his name.

Lord, even when your path takes me through the valley of deepest darkness, fear will never conquer me, for you already have! You remain close to me and lead me through it all the way. Your authority is my strength and my peace.

The comfort of your love takes away my fear. I'll never be lonely, for you are near. You become my delicious feast even when my enemies dare to fight.

You anoint me with the fragrance of your Holy Spirit; you give me all I can drink of you until my heart overflows.

So why would I fear the future? For your goodness and love pursue me all the days of my life." TPT

POSITION YOURSELF FOR SUCCESS

"I have observed something else under the sun. The fastest runner doesn't always win the race, and the strongest warrior doesn't always win the battle.

The wise sometimes go hungry, and the skillful are not necessarily wealthy. And those who are educated don't always lead successful lives.

It is all decided by chance, by being in the right place at the right time." Ecclesiastes 9:11 NLT

This scripture has been a great inspiration and a pillar of hope for me since the days of my youth. Some of us were born with the odds of success stacked against us. If success depended only on speed, strength, wisdom, skill and education, then most of us will never make it! But God in His infinite wisdom and grace levels the playing field to give every person on earth regardless of where they were born, their abilities, skills, gifting or educational background an *equal opportunity* to succeed in this life. **We all have a God-given chance to make something of ourselves whether you were born in Timbuktu or New York City, you were born to Prosper.** You are the Child of the King who equally reigns both in Timbuktu and New York.

Speed, strength, wisdom, skill and education are essential components for success. However, *positioning* is what will decide who succeeds by the end of the day. You have seen fast runners at the Olympics, but there are faster runners out there who can chase and catch an antelope in some African villages. Their problem is where and how they are positioned will never allow them to compete at the Olympics. The point I am making here is that, if you want to succeed, begin to position yourself for success. **Use the in-between seasons to position yourself for victory.** Most people never succeed because when opportunity comes knocking on their door, they are found ill-prepared or indisposed. Some people's opportunity can't even locate them because they are hardly ever where they need to be.

The above scripture gives us three keys for success. But before we get into these keys may I remind you that promotion comes from the LORD and it is God who gives us power to be successful.

> ***"This I know: the favor that brings promotion and power doesn't come from anywhere on earth, for no one exalts a person but God, the true judge of all.***
>
> ***He alone determines where favor rests. He anoints one for greatness and brings another down to his knees."*** Psalm 75:6-7 TPT

> ***"Remember the Lord your God. He is the one who gives you power to be successful, in order to fulfill the covenant he confirmed to your ancestors with an oath."*** Deuteronomy 8:18 NLT

I just want to make sure that you understand that no matter your background, gifting, ability or capacity you are not disadvantaged, God has made sure that you too have an equal opportunity to succeed and prosper. **It is how people position themselves in the in-between seasons, which separates those that excel and establish dynasties from those who settle for subsistence existence.**

FRAME OF MIND

That said, here are the three equalizing keys for positioning yourself for success according to King Solomon in Ecclesiastes 9:11. May I also point out that these keys are not in sequential order. However, they occur, the important thing is that you have the knowledge and understanding.

Chance / Opportunity

As I said earlier, opportunities do come knocking on our doors. It's what we do with these chances and opportunities that makes a difference. ***Most of us are Millionaires in lost opportunities.*** Diligence in stewarding your God-given opportunities is paramount for success. Do not waste your chances because opportunities don't come knocking every day. We are all given chances to make something of ourselves. **The difference however is that while some utilize and capitalize on their chances, others squander their opportunities.**

A lost opportunity is a lost opportunity whatever the reason or excuse you may have. Don't be like the foolish servant who buried his talents. Next time opportunity knocks on your door, may you be found ready!

Being In The Right Place

Positioning yourself in the right place is imperative for success. The right place in this context refers to two aspects of your life. The first aspect I want to discuss is your spiritual, mental and emotional wellbeing. The second is your physical or geographical location. Being in the right place will maximize your potential for success.

Spiritual Alignment

Being in the right place with God positions you in the place of favor with God. The bible says that, ***"And without faith living within us it would be impossible to please God. For we come to God in faith knowing that he is real and that he rewards the faith of those who give all their passion and strength into seeking him."*** Hebrews 11:6 TPT. When we are right with God, we can connect with his purposes and promises. When are our hearts do not condemn us, we can achieve more.

Mental and Emotional Stability

A clear and sober mind is a great asset for success and prosperity. Be in the right frame of mind in order to engaged productively with your chances and opportunities. **Most people are fear driven**

hence they can never step out in faith to cash in their chances.

How we feel emotionally preys a lot on our ability to succeed. If we feel great, we are likely to do better and succeed. When we feel lousy, we are probably more likely to disengage, shutdown or hand in a mediocre performance. The question is, "Where are you, spiritually, mentally and emotionally?"

Right Location

Geography matters! It can either accelerate or inhibit your capacity to succeed and prosper. God wanted to make Abraham into a great nation and make His name famous. But before God could do all this, Abraham had to move from Mesopotamia to Canaan. It may not have been easy leaving all his friends and family behind. Abraham did not allow loyalty to deaden or stand in the way of his future greatness. **I see many people so loyal to dead works that they cannot commit to life and fruitfulness.**

Are you in the right place geographically for your passion and calling to grow? If you are an ice-salesperson, selling ice to Eskimos is not going to make you a fortune. Likewise, if you are a passionate country music singer with a dream to one day make your mark, living in Nashville Tennessee may be an added advantage.

Ever wondered why most people who dream of becoming movie stars relocate to Hollywood?

Right Environment

It is also possible to be in the right place geographically but in the wrong environment. Not every environment is conducive for success and prosperity.

Sometimes you just need to excuse yourself from dysfunctional behaviors and relationships. ***If you were born to soar, spend time with the eagles.*** Where and who you spend your time within the in-between seasons will eventually manifest in your productivity and attitude towards success and prosperity. **Is your environment helping you to achieve your goals and objectives?** If not! Maybe it is time you made some changes.

Right Timing

Timing is critical for success. There is a reason why winter clothes are sold in winter and not in summer. Nature functions in seasons. If you miss your sowing season, you definitely won't have a harvest. It's that simple. The prophet Zechariah in Chapter 10:1 says, ***"Ask the Lord for rain in the spring, for he makes the storm clouds. And he will send showers of rain so every field becomes a lush pasture."*** NLT. Knowing what season and time it is unlocks revelation of what you should be doing and investing in. If it is time for rain, invest in rain!

The sons of Issachar were distinguished by their unique ability to understand and interpret times and seasons. ***"From the tribe of Issachar, there were 200 leaders of the tribe with their relatives. All these men understood the signs of the times and knew the best course for Israel to take."*** 1 Chronicles 12:32 NLT

In the words of Solomon, success is decided by chance, by being in the right place at the right time. We all have the ability to succeed and prosper. It's what we do with our chances and time and how we position ourselves that makes a great difference.

King David fell in sin with Bathsheba and nearly lost his Kingdom because he was not in the right place at a right time. He stayed at home in the season when kings go to war.

> ***"In the spring of the year, when kings normally go out to war, David sent Joab and the Israelite army to fight the Ammonites. They destroyed the Ammonite army and laid siege to the city of Rabbah. However, David stayed behind in Jerusalem.***
>
> ***Late one afternoon, after his midday rest, David got out of bed and was walking on the roof of the palace. As he looked out over the city, he noticed a woman of unusual beauty taking a bath. He sent someone to find out who she was, and he was told, "She is Bathsheba, the daughter of Eliam and the wife of Uriah the Hittite."***
>
> ***Then David sent messengers to get her; and when she came to the palace, he slept with her. She had just completed the purification rites after***

having her menstrual period. Then she returned home.

Later, when Bathsheba discovered that she was pregnant, she sent David a message, saying, "I'm pregnant." 2 Samuel 11:1-5 NLT.

Please refer to your Bible for the rest of this account. There is a lot to learn from it.

Chapter Twelve

Contending For Breakthrough

BEFORE you can take possession of any battle ground you must fight and defeat all other occupying forces. The greatest battle in your life is not out there. It is in your mind.

All battles are fought in two areas: the first is in the spirit realm and the second is in your mind. Any battle you have ever fought or will ever fight will either be won or lost in the spirit and the mind. The good news is that from this moment on you can take this battle to all the enemies of your success and prosperity.

Let's declare war on poverty, mediocrity and apathy. Poverty and lack of money does not glorify God any more than sickness, disease, pain and suffering does.

David had this to say, ***"God, there are two things I'm asking you for before I die, only two: Empty out of my heart everything that is false– every lie, and every crooked thing.***

And give me neither undue poverty nor undue wealth– but rather, feed my soul with the measure of prosperity that pleases you. May my satisfaction be found in you.

Don't let me be so rich that I don't need you or so poor that I have to resort to dishonesty just to make ends meet. Then my life will never detract from bringing glory to your name." Proverbs 30:7-9 TPT

Now, that's a noble thought! Your life is meant to bring glory to God's name. Anything that does not bring glory to God is at war with God. If I am to fight, I choose to fight on God's side, on the side of fruitfulness, increase, multiplication and abundance. On the side of prosperity and good health.

This was John's prayer. ***"Beloved friend, I pray that you are prospering in every way and that you continually enjoy good health, just as your soul is prospering."*** 3 John 1:2 TPT. This is an involuntary war, like it or not you are in it. The world all around you is a manifestation of our thoughts and whatever is established in the spirit ream. We can either align ourselves with God and release good or the enemy and release bad.

"Receive this truth: Whatever you forbid on earth will be considered to be forbidden in heaven, and whatever you release on earth will be considered to be released in heaven.

Again, I give you an eternal truth: If two of you agree to ask God for something in a symphony of prayer, my heavenly Father will do it for you. For wherever two or three come together in honor of my name, I am right there with them!" Matthew 18:18-20 TPT

FIRST AGREE WITH GOD

You and I have a great part to play. We literally affect heaven and earth by our thoughts, attitudes and the words we say. Your words have creative power and your thoughts become things.

By your words you give or deny permission to entities in the spirit realm. You have the ability to shape the landscape of your world. The best place to start from is to deny the enemy by agreeing with God. You defeat the spirit of poverty by embracing God's prosperity. Any spiritual battle has to be won in the spiritual ream. Paul wrote this to the Church in Corinth;

"For although we live in the natural realm, we don't wage a military campaign employing human weapons, using manipulation to achieve our aims. Instead, our spiritual weapons are energized with divine power to effectively dismantle the defenses behind which people hide.

We can demolish every deceptive fantasy that opposes God and break through every arrogant attitude that is raised up in defiance of the true knowledge of God. We capture, like prisoners of war, every thought and insist that it bow in obedience to the Anointed One.

Since we are armed with such dynamic weaponry, we stand ready to punish any trace of rebellion, as soon as you choose complete obedience." 2 Corinthians 10:4-6 TPT

For some people despite their best efforts, they just don't seem to have a breakthrough. They move three steps forward and four steps back. They work very hard but never get ahead. They can never keep anything they acquire; they feel as though there is a hidden force at work against them or just plain bad luck. If this sounds like you, maybe there is indeed a hidden force undermining your efforts. **It might be time to pray and break that spiritual assignment against you in the heavenly places.** If there is a pattern of what I described in your family, it could be that there is a generational bondage. Ask someone to agree with you in prayer to break any generational curses and assignments. The spirit world is more real than the natural world. What happens in the spirit has far reaching impact and consequences than you realize. If it wasn't so Jesus would not have said, ***"Whatever you forbid on earth will be considered to be forbidden in heaven, and whatever you release on earth will***

be considered to be released in heaven." Matthew 18:18 TPT

TAKING THOUGHTS CAPTIVE

The second part is taking thoughts opposed to God captive. You cannot afford to have any thoughts which are contrary to God's thoughts.

If thoughts become things, then there is great need to keep your thoughts in check. Take a proactive stance not to entertain negative thinking and negative people. Most people are defeated even before the battle has begun. **You have to win the war in your mind before you can win in reality.**

Begin to see yourself as having already arrived at a place you want to be. Romans 4:17 TPT makes this statement, ***"God can raise the dead and call into being things that don't even exist yet."*** God sees you in the fullness of what He made you to be. In God's eyes you are already there. Begin to think, see, behave as the person God made you to be. **Sometimes you just have to fake it until your circumstances catch up with who you were born to be.**

I find this passage of scripture very encouraging, ***"I make known the end from the beginning, from ancient times, what is still to come. I say, 'My purpose will stand, and I will do all that I please.' From the east I summon a bird of prey; from a far-off land, a man to fulfill my purpose. What I have said, that I will bring about; what I have planned, that I will do."*** Isaiah 46:10-11 NIV

This is so incredible that God has established the end of your life from the beginning. That means that God has got you covered from start to end. As far as He is concerned you are a winner, so begin to think like a winner.

"A final word: Be strong in the Lord and in his mighty power. Put on all of God's armor so that you will be able to stand firm against all strategies of the devil.

For we are not fighting against flesh-and-blood enemies, but against evil rulers and authorities of the unseen world, against mighty powers in this dark world, and against evil spirits in the heavenly places.

Therefore, put on every piece of God's armor so you will be able to resist the enemy in the time of evil. Then after the battle you will still be standing firm.

Stand your ground, putting on the belt of truth and the body armor of God's righteousness. For shoes, put on the peace that comes from the Good News so that you will be fully prepared. In addition to all of these, hold up the shield of faith to stop the fiery arrows of the devil.

Put on salvation as your helmet, and take the sword of the Spirit, which is the word of God. Pray in the Spirit at all times and on every occasion. Stay alert and be persistent in your prayers for all believers everywhere." Ephesians 6:10-18 NLT

PRAYER AND FASTING

Whenever you can't see a breakthrough in your life, escalate the fight in the Spirit by prayer and fasting. Prayer will keep you connected to the heart of God and fasting will keep you humble.

The point is that there is more to living a successful life beyond planning and hard work. If it is God who gives you the strength to produce wealth, then staying engaged in the spiritual ream is never a bad idea.

If you are not seeing results, don't give up. Keep pushing and contending for breakthrough. The darkest hour is often before dawn. Remember, with God on your side who can be against you? ***"So, what does all this mean? If God has determined to stand with us, tell me, who then could ever stand against us?"*** Romans 8:31 TPT

KNOCKED DOWN, BUT NOT OUT

You may be feeling like Paul in 2 Corinthians 4:9 TPT, ***"We are persecuted by others, but God has not forsaken us. We may be knocked down, but not out."***

Whatever the circumstance no matter how bad it may be, it will pass! You may be falling down, but you are certainly not out. Never write yourself off or allow people to write you off. **You may have fallen behind but you are definitely still in the race!**

Be confident, believe in yourself. Discard any lies of the enemy over your life. Don't let unbelief and self-doubt rob you of your victory. A positive and healthy self-image will go a long way in your journey to success and prosperity.

Poverty mentality is not your friend. Remove any cobwebs from your mind.

Chapter Thirteen

COMMUNICATING YOUR DREAM

YOUR choices and decisions have a great impact on the lives of the people you care about.

This makes communicating your dream very imperative. Whatever you decide to do, you will either get a reaction or a response from them.

The how and when: CONVICTION

Therefore, how and when you communicate is equally as important as the dream. A dream effectively communicated will more likely solicit a desired response.

Think of your dream as a product for sale. Your goal is to convince the people in your life to believe not only in you but in your dream also. If you can convince people to believe, they will buy into your dream. This is when your dream becomes their dream as well. People will be willing to stand and fight with you and for you to achieve your dreams. It's more than having a good idea that would rally people to gravitate towards you and your dreams. People will be compelled by your drive and passion. Exhibit enough confidence and conviction to make the sceptics reconsider their position. To turn your dream into reality, you will need to have enough faith to believe for both yourself and your critics.

The why: MOBILISATION

There are several reasons why it is important to communicate your dream. Like I said earlier, your choices and decisions affect people you care about. It is honoring to keep them involved and informed;

it is just good manners. The people in your life are already vested in you, therefore you owe them a little bit of a heads up. Sharing your dream with people close to you will more likely provide you with some objective and candid feedback. Because not only do they know your potential, but they also know areas where you would require help and support. **Communicating your dream mobilizes a squad of cheerleaders on your side of the arena.** From a business point of view, you will need people's assistance to implement your dream and ideas.

KEYS TO COMMUNICATING YOUR DREAM

In order to sell your dream and ideas, effective communication is of the essence. You will have to be precise and concise. The purpose of communication is to paint a vibrant audible word picture for people to see what you mean and hear what you are saying without getting lost in the process and details. It is saying what you mean to say exactly how you mean to say it. If there is no discrepancy between the words out of your mouth and the words people hear, then you have done your job well. If your words can become alive to give your listeners a precise and concise picture of what is in your mind, then you have communicated effectively. **The reason for most fallouts between people is poor communication.**

Misunderstanding is a fruit of poor communication. Whenever there is a case of misunderstanding, it is never the fault of the listener but the communicator. As a communicator it is your responsibility to ensure that your listeners hear exactly what you want them to hear in a precise manor you want them to hear. I am not talking about manipulating people. I am saying that in your communication there should not be any ambiguity that leaves any doubts, question or second guessing to your hearers about what you said. **Communication is an art!** Those who fail to master this art will be victims of misunderstanding and misinterpretation. Better communication means better relationships, maximum productivity and less time spent clarifying statements and apologizing because we misspoke.

KEY #1: TIMING

A great idea communicated at a wrong time is as good as a bad idea communicated at the right time. I have three brilliant children; they are all full of energy and have great ideas which they are keen to share with me. But I find whenever they try to share their ideas with me when I am in the middle of doing something else, they usually don't get the desired response they are looking for. In those instances, I could see their frustration because they didn't feel listened to.

My point is, learn to pick your timing. This shows the people you are pitching to that you value and appreciate their time. It also helps people to focus and listen to you objectively without being distracted. If you don't pick the right timing you risk being viewed as a nuisance, this will definitely not help your cause.

Four Factors to Right Timing

1. Right Place

I use the word **"place"** in a broad sense. This could be a particular position in views, thoughts, ideas and philosophy, point, or a location as in office, restaurant or home. **Share your ideas at the place most conducive for the desired effect.** Some people may not like discussing business at dinner or family events. Know your audience!

2. Right Conditions

I don't suppose summer is the best time to sell winter jackets. You may have a great idea but if the conditions aren't right, you are more likely to have opposition or experience some rejection. Right conditions are like the weather. When it's all right the farmer will take his chances and plant the seed or otherwise will hold-off until the conditions change.

3. Right Atmosphere

The right atmosphere has great impact on people's reactions and responses. It takes the edge off any sense of awkwardness. When the atmosphere is tense, it could be a good idea to wait until things cool down. When your boss is stressed about something, it may not be the right atmosphere to ask for a pay-raise. It's like a girl really busting to go to the bathroom and the boy decides to stage a grand proposal with the mariachi performance. **Every successful hunt lies in the ability to pick the right moment.**

4. Right Mood

A mood is a temporary state of mind or feeling. This gives you an insight on what someone is feeling and how they are likely to react to what you have to say. If someone appears to be in a very good mood, it may be assumed that he or she is in a better frame of mind or state of mind to emotionally respond rationally to your proposal.

If someone seems to be in an angry, irritable, or sullen state of mind they are probably in a bad mood. It may be best to wait for another opportune time.

KEY #2: WISDOM

When and how you communicate your dream will have a great bearing on the outcome. Wisdom exhibits good judgement. It helps people determine whether you have the necessary skills, knowledge and maturity to perform at the expected level.

Wisdom will help you gain people's trust and confidence. Look at Proverbs 9:10 NLT, ***"Fear of the Lord is the foundation of wisdom. Knowledge of the Holy One results in good judgment." "Where can wisdom be found? It is born in the fear of God.***

Everyone who follows his ways Will never lack his living-understanding. And the adoration of God Will abide throughout eternity!" Psalm 111:10 TPT

"And if anyone longs to be wise, ask God for wisdom and he will give it! He won't see your lack of wisdom as an opportunity to scold you over your failures but he will overwhelm your failures with his generous grace." James 1:5 TPT

KEY #3: ASSOCIATION

The third key to communicating your dream is **who** you talk to.

Pearls are not for pigs! ***"Who would hang earrings on a dog's ear or throw pearls in front of wild pigs? They'll only trample them under their feet and then turn around and tear you to pieces!"*** ~ Matthew 7:6 TPT.

Talk to mature and objective people. People who will give you Godly counsel and tell you both what you need to hear and what you don't want to hear. Talk to people that would seek God's heart for you rather than push their own agenda and opinions.

Avoid the "glass-half-empty" type of people ~ those who find a problem in everything who sow seeds of doubt and discouragement.

They will kill your dream; they are the kind of people who love to give advice to everyone but receive none from anyone. While I appreciate that every idea has two sides, cons and pros, they have to be both weighed in order to find the best possible way forward. It takes a real treasure-hunter to find a gem hidden in the rough. **Such people are rare, they help you to see past your faults, failures and limitations.** They just don't see who you are, but they also see who you *can* be. They invest in your life in order to maximize your potential, talents and abilities. They are people who will stand by you regardless of the situation or circumstances. These are the people who love you and believe in you. When everybody quits on you, they are the only ones left still standing in your corner. These are the people you want to share your dreams with!

Most people are like vultures, only interested to pick at the carcass of dead dreams. They are self-righteous and take so much pleasure in saying, "I told you so". They find a sense of gratification when their doom prophecy manifests. This also means they are not likely to celebrate your achievements.

Chapter Fourteen

KEYS TO LIVING YOUR DREAM

THANK God for Thomas Jefferson and his vision and inspiration of, "Life, Liberty and the Pursuit of Happiness". These are words that remain immortalized in the USA constitution, words which have inspired people from all walks of life to seek a better life for themselves. These words make me believe that if we work very hard, we can have our dreams come true.

But somehow, I wonder what the pursuit of happiness meant to Mr. Jefferson. Did it mean the same thing it means to you and me today?

It seems to me that for most of us the pursuit of happiness looks like a dog chasing its tail. We are running around in circles chasing an illusion.

WHAT EXACTLY IS HAPPINESS?

A Common Viewpoint:

I tried searching the web dictionaries to find the definition of happiness but felt more confused than ever. It seems the meaning varies depending on your philosophy and background. Here is what I mean; *"Happiness is that feeling that comes over you when you know life is good and you can't help but smile. It's the opposite of sadness. Happiness is a sense of well-being, joy, or contentment. When people are successful, or safe, or lucky, they feel happiness."* https:// www.vocabulary.com

"In psychology, happiness is a mental or emotional state of well-being which can be defined by, among others, positive or pleasant emotions ranging from contentment to intense joy. Happy mental states may reflect judgements by a person about their overall wellbeing." https://en.wikipedia.org/wiki/Happiness

These are just two samples among many definitions. However, the common thread is that happiness is caused by what *happens* to you. It's driven by circumstances. When something good happens, you are happy and when something bad happens then you are sad. This idea of happiness is like a rollercoaster. Nobody can thus ever truly be happy; you can easily lose your happiness with the change of circumstances. People can give you happiness or make you happy just as easily as they can take away your happiness or make you sad. I don't think this is the way for people to live.

The modern take on the pursuit of happiness is based on acquiring wealth and fortune, but is this what it really means to be happy? I must admit that wealth does help make living comfortable, but it doesn't bring happiness.

If it were so, why do wealthy people commit suicide? I use the statement, "wealth does help make living comfortable" because many people live comfortably but do not necessarily have a happy life.

The Biblical Perspective

The Bible reveals happiness is *self-contained.* **It's something within you, not something that happens to you.** This is particularly good because nothing and nobody can ever take away your happiness. Regardless of our station in life, we are all equally privileged because we all have happiness within us, we can all live our dream. **Happiness is no longer an unattainable illusion but a reality within our grasp.** All we must do is to look deep within ourselves.

PURSUE GOD'S PURPOSE FOR YOUR LIFE

Happiness is linked to your *purpose and destiny* rather than your possessions. You will draw much joy, fulfilment and satisfaction in having accomplished your purpose than in all the wealth you can ever muster.

You were born for a purpose, there is a gap in your heart which can only be filled by fulfilling the purpose you were born for. **There is a natural longing in your heart which pulls and compels you to walk on the path of your destiny.** The further you drift from this path, the more unsatisfying and unfulfilling your life will become. You begin to experience this hollow feeling which leads into depression.

This explains why someone can be rich but still struggle with depression. It's because deep inside the heart, there is a longing to reconnect to the divine purpose they were born for. This hole can't be filled with money, drugs, sex, alcohol or any other pacification of choice. It's a "GOD" shaped hole only God can fill.

You were born to exist in *communion* with God. Your life is meant to be a mirror and reflection of the fullness of God. Acts 17:28-30 TPT puts it this way, ***"It is through him that we live and function and have our identity; just as your own poets have said, 'Our lineage comes from him.'***

"Since our lineage can be traced back to God, how could we even think that the divine image could be compared to something made of gold, silver, or stone, sculpted by man's artwork and clever imagination?

"In the past God tolerated our ignorance of these things, but now the time of deception has passed away. He commands us all to repent and turn to God."

Your purpose and fulfilment are *in God*. When we fail to purse a relationship with God we end up with religion. In religion you will always be seeking and searching without achieving contentment. Listen to this, ***"Now when David had served God's purpose in his own generation, he fell asleep; he was buried with his ancestors and his body decayed."*** Acts 13:36 NIV.

You were born to *serve* God's purpose in your *generation*. This is the key to true happiness, everything else is merely a bonus. ***"Eternal life means to know and experience you as the only true God, and to know and experience Jesus Christ, as the Son whom you have sent."*** John 17:3 TPT.

If you really want to be happy, *fall in love* with God, ***"What bliss we experience when these blessings fall! The people who love and serve our God will be happy indeed!"*** Psalm 144:15 TPT.

"Make God the utmost delight and pleasure of your life, and he will provide for you what you desire the most. Give God the right to direct your life, and as you trust him along the way you'll find he pulled it off perfectly!" Psalm 37:4-5 TPT

THE RESULT OF GODLY HAPPINESS

Prosperity is a fruit of following God. ***"So above all, constantly chase after the realm of God's kingdom and the righteousness that proceeds from him. Then all these less important things will be given to you abundantly."*** Matthew 6:33 TPT.

Remember Deuteronomy 28:1-7 NLT ***"If you fully obey the Lord your God and carefully keep all his commands that I am giving you today, the Lord your God will set you high above all the nations of the world.***

You will experience all these blessings if you obey the Lord your God: Your towns and your fields will be blessed. Your children and your crops will be blessed.

The offspring of your herds and flocks will be blessed. Your fruit baskets and breadboards will be blessed. Wherever you go and whatever you do, you will be blessed.

"The Lord will conquer your enemies when they attack you. They will attack you from one direction, but they will scatter from you in seven!"

DEFINING YOUR DRIVE

Identifying your *passion* is a good place to start from. What's your drive? What *compels* you in the morning to get out of bed to do what you do? Your compelling drive is a great force which will propel you from where you are to where you need to be. It gives you focus and motivation to keep pushing through against the current towards your dream.

Your drive is a *battle cry* which summons every ounce of energy within you to reach your goal. It's your rallying cause. Find your compelling drive, be committed and dedicated to your dream. Stay focused, don't toss back and forth like the waves at the sea. Without a compelling drive you are like a high-performance vehicle without fuel, you are going nowhere. Don't have a *"whatever-goes attitude"*. You are better than this. Live your life purposefully, make every moment count.

Aim for something, shoot for the stars. This is the issue with most people, they do not have a compelling cause in their lives. Hence, they live life aimlessly without a target to aim for. Without a goal you are like an airplane flying around without a heading or destination. You may fly high, but you are just going around in circles. Don't allow people to tell you what you can and can't do. **Believe in your dream and defy people's expectations.** Astound not only the pessimists, but equally blow the minds of the optimists as well.

Defining your drive helps you to determine and *reach* your objectives. Perhaps one of the errors of modern society is the elimination of healthy *competition* in schools and play grounds. We no longer keep score at games because we don't want to destroy the kids' confidence if they lose but somehow, we still expect these same kids to grow up and win gold medals at the Olympics.

Schools don't give **"F"** grade for fail because it could impact self-esteem, they use letters like **"E"** for effort or encouragement. I look at a school report and everything is coded. I need a manual to help me understand exactly how my children are performing at school.

RELOOK AT AMBITION

There is a generation leaving universities today which is totally unprepared for the real world and work place. All we have managed to do is raise a generation of people without passion, drive and ambition. I still talk to adults who are confused and frustrated because they still don't know what they want to do in life.

A little ambition will take you a long way. You cannot achieve an equal opportunity society by cutting the heads off the tall poppies. Neither can you build the esteem and confidence of someone by denigrating the capability and beliefs of others. Fairness does not mean uniformity.

This is the ethos of communism! ***"You cannot strengthen one by weakening the other, and you cannot add to the stature of a dwarf by cutting off the legs of a giant."*** Benjamin Franklin

Most of us struggle with the word **"ambition"** because we have been raised to think of ambition as a dirty word. Hence, I have opted to using the phrase **"Compelling Drive."** Defining your compiling drive is the basis for making choices, decisions and preparations for the future. Unless you know where you are going and the expected conditions, how do you know what to pack? The future is now! What you do today will determine what you become tomorrow. If you don't do today what needs doing today, when tomorrow comes you will be a day behind. This is the reason why most people never get ahead. Procrastination is adversarial to your dreams. Be proactive, don't hold back, pursue your dream, be all you can be and fulfil God's purpose on your life. **Live for something bigger than yourself and your immediate needs.**

INVEST IN YOURSELF

Do for yourself what only you can do for yourself. Too often we wait and look to others for a breakthrough, while God has put within us everything, we need to make our dream come true. After all it's your dream, it's your responsibility to make it happen.

You must believe in yourself and your dream more than anybody else. **You must be willing make sacrifices and do whatever it takes to achieve your dream.**

Too many people want a free ride and are not willing to pay the price. The man on top of the mountain had to walk there one step at a time till he reached the summit. He had to overcome exhaustion, fatigue, hunger and resist every urge to give up. **When you succeed on the unbeaten path, you become a trailblazer, a shining example and a great hope and inspiration to generations.**

Not until 1953 when Tenzing Norgay and Edmund Hillary made the first successful official climb to the summit of Mount Everest, was it deemed as possible. They overcame altitude sickness to achieve the impossible. Their success made the world to believe that climbing Mount Everest was achievable. Since then more than 4,000 have conquered the mountain and reached the summit of Mount Everest.

Before the Wright brothers made that first flight in human history on December 17th, 1903 the world didn't think flying was possible. They may have only flown for 20 feet, but today man has flown to the moon and back. The Wright brothers ignited a flicker of imagination and possibilities which gave birth to modern global air travel.

Invest in your dream by making adequate preparations. Things just don't happen, failing to plan is planning to fail. Educate yourself, read some books, take a self-help course. **Education is the greatest investment you can ever make in yourself.** Whichever way you learn best, whether you are a bookworm or streetwise continue developing and improving yourself and skills. Allocate all the necessary resources required for you to fulfil your dream.

JOY AND CONTENTMENT

"I'm not telling you this because I'm in need, for I have learned to be satisfied in any circumstance.

I know what it means to lack, and I know what it means to experience overwhelming abundance.

For I'm trained in the secret of overcoming all things, whether in fullness or in hunger.

And I find that the strength of Christ's explosive power infuses me to conquer every difficulty." Philippians 4:11-13 TPT.

Pursuing your dreams and being content may sound contradictory, but satisfaction and contentment comes as a result of having fulfilled your dream and purpose.

GOD'S HEART IS SERVING PEOPLE

God instilled that dream in you. The dream that God has given you is not self-seeking or serving, it lays a path which leads *back* to God's heart.

It's impossible to succeed without touching and impacting the lives of people around you. True success is only achieved by serving and meeting the felt needs of people. When you meet the needs of people, you are touching God's heart. The matrix of success and prosperity is the more people you can serve the more successful and prosperous you become.

This is the reason why God wants you to be prosperous. **God knows that if you are to pursue wealth and riches, you must first pursue serving people.** You must balance the equation between service output and reward input or returns. The more you serve the more you will be rewarded, It's that simple!

Most rich, wealthy, successful and prosperous people and businesses have mastered the art of serving people. They have either created a service or product which has made people's lives better, easier or fun. People enjoy and appreciate these services and products so much that they are willing to pay a lot of money to receive these services and products. Apple creates these wonderful gadgets that people all over world queue in lines over night outside braving the cold. These people pay a lot of money just to have the latest gadget.

Think of Skype, Facebook, Instagram and many other services which we all love to use. Those people who created these services and products became instant billionaires. ***The secret to wealth creation and prosperity is not pursuing money but pursuing excellence in the services and products which people are willing to pay for."*** This is called Branding. We will discuss more about this in the chapter, "The art of Success".

"My fellow believers, when it seems as though you are facing nothing but difficulties see it as an invaluable opportunity to experience the greatest joy that you can!

For you know that when your faith is tested it stirs up power within you to endure all things. And then as your endurance grows even stronger it will release perfection into every part of your being until there is nothing missing and nothing lacking." James 1:2-4 TPT

PATIENCE & ENDURANCE

Be patient, Rome was not built in a day. Develop endurance, all good things take time. God doesn't just want you to get to the top. He wants you to stay on top. It's character and patient endurance that gives you the wisdom to succeed where others may have failed. ***"Let joy be your continual feast. Make your life a prayer. And in the midst of everything be always giving thanks, for this is God's perfect plan for you in Christ Jesus.***

Never restrain or put out the fire of the Holy Spirit. And don't be one who scorns prophecies but be faithful to examine them by putting them to the test, and afterward hold tightly to what has proven to be right. Avoid every appearance of evil." 1Thessalonians 5:16-22 TPT

Develop a solid prayer life. Remember every battle in your life has to be won in the spirit realm before it can manifest in the natural. A life of prayer keeps you engaged with the heart, wisdom and counsel of God. Prayer also helps you to maintain a good perspective between your challenges and the faithfulness and greatness of God.

SURRENDER

Surrender yourself to the leading of the Holy Spirit. If you do, you will discover Psalm 23 TPT first hand, ***"The Lord is my best friend and my shepherd. I always have more than enough. He offers a resting place for me in his luxurious love.***

His tracks take me to an oasis of peace, the quiet brook of bliss. That's where he restores and revives my life.

He opens before me pathways to God's pleasure and leads me along in his footsteps of righteousness so that I can bring honor to his name.

Lord, even when your path takes me through the valley of deepest darkness, fear will never conquer me, for you already have! You remain close to me and lead me through it all the way.

Your authority is my strength and my peace. The comfort of your love takes away my fear. I'll never be lonely, for you are near. You become my delicious feast even when my enemies dare to fight.

You anoint me with the fragrance of your Holy Spirit; you give me all I can drink of you until my heart overflows.

So why would I fear the future? For your goodness and love pursue me all the days of my life. Then afterward, when my life is through, I'll return to your glorious presence to be forever with you!"

DON'T BUILD ON QUICK SAND

"Everyone who hears my teaching and applies it to his life can be compared to a wise man who built his house on an unshakable foundation. When the rains fell and the flood came, with fierce winds beating upon his house, it stood firm because of its strong foundation.

"But everyone who hears my teaching and does not apply it to his life can be compared to a foolish man who built his house on sand. When it rained and rained and the flood came, with wind and waves beating upon his house, it collapsed and was swept away." Matthew 7:24-27 TPT

Don't build your life on people's perception of you. Teach people how to treat you by being true to who you are and God's calling on your life. **Set out to build God's dream and God will build your dream.** Focus on truth, don't build on lies either your own or other people's.

Popular myths are still myths, don't waste your time with them. Here is an old classic, "Everyone is doing it," So what? You are not everyone. Learn from people who have gone before you and you will do well.

Chapter Fifteen

Success is a Symphony

SUCCESS is a symphony, it's not a solo act. We are all just one small part of the grand orchestra. The majesty and beauty of it all depends on a collective of individual outstanding performances culminating in one masterful work of art. **We all bring and add value to one another.** Every cog in a great machine needs to function as intended otherwise that piece of machinery will not have optimum performance and productivity. It's like a human body, every part is significant.

"The human body has many parts, but the many parts make up one whole body. So it is with the body of Christ. Some of us are Jews, some are Gentiles, some are slaves, and some are free. But we have all been baptized into one body by one Spirit, and we all share the same Spirit.

Yes, the body has many different parts, not just one part. If the foot says, "I am not a part of the body because I am not a hand," that does not make it any less a part of the body.

And if the ear says, "I am not part of the body because I am not an eye," would that make it any less a part of the body? If the whole body were an eye, how would you hear? Or if your whole body were an ear, how would you smell anything?

But our bodies have many parts, and God has put each part just where he wants it. How strange a body would be if it had only one part! Yes, there are many parts, but only one body. The eye can never say to the hand, "I don't need you." The head can't say to the feet, "I don't need you."

In fact, some parts of the body that seem weakest and least important are actually the most necessary.

And the parts we regard as less honorable are those we clothe with the greatest care. So we carefully protect those parts that should not be seen, while the more honorable parts do not require this special care.

So God has put the body together such that extra honor and care are given to those parts that have less dignity. This makes for harmony among the members, so that all the members care for each other.

If one part suffers, all the parts suffer with it, and if one part is honored, all the parts are glad. All of you together are Christ's body, and each of you is a part of it." 1 Corinthians 12:12-27 NLT

The point here is that you can't make it on your own, you need what others carry. Other people have the gifting, abilities, skills, experience and knowledge necessary for your success. **A mark of wisdom and character lies in your ability to identify people pertinent to your success.**

RELATIONSHIPS CONTRIBUTE TO SUCCESS

There are four types of relationships in your life I would like to discuss.

1. FAMILY

They say, "you can't choose your family!" **But you can certainly choose *how* to engage and interact with them.** Like I said in the chapter "Communicating your Dream", family is part of your life for better or worse. At one point or another you may need to call on them or they will call on you. Don't hang on to grievances, keep a short account of offences.

2. COMRADERY

This is the most common relationship. Comradery is a spirit of friendship and sense of community where you are celebrated as part of the group of family. These are people we seem to spend most of our time with, be it at school, work, church and other social activities. This is the group of people which has a great deal of influence in our lives.

They influence our fashion, morals, values, choices and decisions.

Take care who you admit to this special group of people in your life because you will end up looking exactly like them. Choose your friends wisely, unless you want for yourself the same as your friends, it might be time for a new set of influencers. **You are either influencing or being influenced, which one are you?**

3. ZERO-SUM

These are draining relationships; they keep on taking and taking but never add any value to your life. They could be very time and energy consuming without any sense of real accomplishment by the end of the day. They can be very negative and discouraging, they manage to see the worst in everything. They are like Eeyore, the Winnie-the-Pooh character. He is always pessimistic, depressed, gloomy and anhedonic, he can't find any pleasure or fun in anything! **This is the kind of relationship where you always have to be a hero doing all the heavy lifting.**

You receive very little gratitude and a lot of criticism when you fail to meet their need or expectation. They are a leaking bucket which can never be filled. What they need is divine intervention.

4. DESTINY BEARING

The fourth type of relationship is rare and very far apart in-between. This is the relationship like Frodo and Sam, like Jonathan and David.

"After David had finished talking with Saul, Jonathan became one in spirit with David, and he loved him as himself. From that day Saul kept David with him and did not let him return home to his family. And Jonathan made a covenant with David because he loved him as himself.

Jonathan took off the robe he was wearing and gave it to David, along with his tunic, and even his sword, his bow and his belt. Whatever mission Saul sent him on, David was so successful that Saul gave him a high rank in the army. This pleased all the troops, and Saul's officers as well." 1 Samuel 18:1-5 NIV

These sorts of relationships come in the form of covenant or divine connections. They are relationships which have a bearing on your purpose and destiny. **They are a divine providence orchestrated to set you up for a breakthrough.** Every now and then, God brings people in your life who touch you in a way that nothing is ever the same again. **These door-openers are very easy to miss because they don't come announced.** Most often we are too distracted by the other three relationships mentioned above that we fail to notice our moment of visitation. **Certain people you have an intertwined destiny with, these are relationships you ought to treasure and invest in.** Don't miss your opportunity, do whatever you need to walk through any open-door God sets before you.

WISDOM

An African proverb says, ***"Wisdom is like a baobab tree; no one individual can embrace it."*** Here is my personal favorite, ***"A fool is in love with his own opinion, but wisdom means being teachable."*** Psalm 12:15 TPT.

You can try to do things alone, but you won't get far. When you walk with others, it might take a little bit longer, but you will definitely get there! Insisting on doing things your own way and by yourself is a typical trait found in toddlers. "No mommy, I want to do it myself". Such behaviour has its uses in your development, but accepting help is a sign of maturity and asking for help is a mark of wisdom.

RELATIONSHIP SKILLS

If success is a symphony, then developing relationship skills is a must. Interpersonal skills are an art which can be learnt by anyone.

Make an effort to relate and connect with people. Don't be one of those people who sit in a corner because nobody is talking to them. You never know which conversation will lead to an open door of opportunity. You may identify yourself as, "not a people person" but this is a lie, there is no such thing. **There are only *loving* people!** All you have to do is take interest in the person in front of you. Of course, there are extroverts and introverts, but what does that have to do with loving?

In fact, being an introvert can be an advantage because you can listen more, observe and see more. This will give you an edge to connect with people on a deeper level than the mundane superficial interactions.

INTEGRITY

> ***"A beautiful reputation is more to be desired than great riches, and to be esteemed by others is more honorable than to own immense investments."*** Proverbs 22:1 TPT.

These words were written by King Solomon, the richest man that has ever walked the surface of the earth. I think he knows what he is talking about. Let your words be your bond, do what you say you will do and your word will be as good as cash. That's how business deals on a hand-shake worked. ***"Now stand up for me and don't let me fall, for I've walked with integrity."*** Psalm 41:12 TPT

BE HONEST

Nobody wants to get involved with a shady person. Establish a reputation of honesty and integrity. People would rather pay a little bit more for excellent services than deal with people of questionable character and ethics. Let integrity and honesty be your trademark. Here is some advice from a wise King, ***"What you obtain dishonestly may seem sweet at first, but sooner or later you'll live to regret it."*** Proverbs 20:17 TPT

DEPENDABILITY

My mother would say to me, ***"The sharpest axe suffers the most!"*** This was her way of telling me that she appreciated my impeccable performance in all chores she asked me to do. She would always count on me if she needed a job well done ~ I was her sharpest axe. Many times, it felt like she was picking on me. She taught me, **"If you are dependable, people will always seek you out for things that really matter to them."**

I came to fully appreciate mom's proverb through this scripture, ***"In a wealthy home some utensils are made of gold and silver, and some are made of wood and clay. The expensive utensils are used for special occasions, and the cheap ones are for everyday use.***

If you keep yourself pure, you will be a special utensil for honorable use. Your life will be clean, and you will be ready for the Master to use you for every good work." 2 Timothy 2:20-21 NLT

The choice and decision is yours to make on what type of utensil you would like to be. ***"Always be eager to present yourself before God as a perfect and mature minister, without shame, as one who correctly explains the Word of Truth."*** 2 Timothy 2:15 TPT 172

WALK WITH PEOPLE GOING THE SAME DIRECTION AS YOURSELF

Birds of a feather flock together.

"Can two people walk together without agreeing on the direction?" Amos 3:3 NLT.

Two people can't walk together unless they agree. Don't get derailed and sidetracked or led astray by time-wasters. If you find people headed the same direction as you, there are great benefits to be had.

"Two people are better off than one, for they can help each other succeed. If one person falls, the other can reach out and help. But someone who falls alone is in real trouble.

Likewise, two people lying close together can keep each other warm. But how can one be warm alone? A person standing alone can be attacked and defeated, but two can stand back-to-back and conquer. Three are even better, for a triple-braided cord is not easily broken." Ecclesiastes 4:9-12 NLT

DON'T BE DOUBLE-MINDED

> ***"If you need wisdom, ask our generous God, and he will give it to you. He will not rebuke you for asking. But when you ask him, be sure that your faith is in God alone.***

Do not waver, for a person with divided loyalty is as unsettled as a wave of the sea that is blown and tossed by the wind.

Such people should not expect to receive anything from the Lord. Their loyalty is divided between God and the world, and they are unstable in everything they do." *James 1:5-8*

ON YOUR WAY UP

In Africa it is said, ***"On your way up a fruit tree, don't forget the people you are leaving below. Should you fall, they would be the ones to catch and break your fall."*** I guess this means that on your way up the ladder of success, make the lives of people around you better.

I read a story of a man who became wealthy and retired early. He bought all the toys a young retired man could need. One problem though, he became very lonely because all his friends were always out to work earning a living. He couldn't go golfing or boating by himself. What if he had shared his strategy of success with some of his friends. Maybe he could have taken them with himself up the ladder of success. Then maybe they could all have retired together and gone golfing, fishing, boating or whatever bored rich people do together, just maybe!

Chapter Sixteen

YOUR GREATEST ASSETS

1. YOUR MIND

Your mind has an infinite capacity to imagine. Think of all the advances in modern technology, they all came out of someone's imagination. Whatever you can conceive in your mind has the potential to take physical shape and form.

Unfortunately for the majority of us this creative part of life has been shut down because we were told to stop daydreaming. Let me help you, God has the most imaginative mind ever! I mean how does someone think of creating a Pink Fairy

Armadillo, Dumbo Octopus, or a Blob Fish for that matter? The reason why daydreaming is discouraged is because *people have misunderstood the difference between an idle mind and daydreaming*. Wishful thinking is also probably something you got in trouble for. I have good news for you, I highly recommend wishful thinking and daydreaming. First let me explain a few things.

An idle mind is synonymous with unproductively. It's when you are doing nothing while thinking that you should be doing something. It is a blank space waiting to be filled and that's what makes it the devil's workshop.

Wishful Thinking

Wishful thinking is peeking through the keyhole of possibilities. The problem is that most people merely peek. **Wishful thinking ignites hope, those who peek long enough develop a desire to find a way in.** History has proven that where there is hope there is a will and where there is a will there is a way.

Daydreaming

Daydreaming is when you let your mind wander into the past, present and future to explore alternative realities and solutions. This is the realm where mind-blowing innovations, discoveries and inventions are found. This is where we get a glimpse of what can be and this ignites faith in our spirit to believe God for the impossible. Most of my daydreams became my dreams which turned into potential which has finally manifested into reality.

Daydreaming is God's invitation to Faith! If you can see it, you can believe it. If you can believe it, you can have it. Let's assume for a second that we truly believed that, ***"Every Scripture has been written by the Holy Spirit, the breath of God. It will empower you by its instruction and correction, giving you the strength to take the right direction and lead you deeper into the path of godliness. Then you will be God's servant, fully mature and perfectly prepared to fulfill any assignment God gives you."*** 2 Timothy 3:16-17 TPT.

Then we might perhaps believe and accept this part of scripture 1 Corinthians 2:11-16 TPT ***"After all, who can really see into a person's heart and know his hidden impulses except for that person's spirit? So it is with God. His thoughts and secrets are only fully understood by his Spirit, the Spirit of God.***

For we did not receive the spirit of this world system but the Spirit of God, so that we might come to understand and experience all that grace has lavished upon us. And we articulate these realities with the words imparted to us by the Spirit and not with the words taught by human wisdom.

We join together Spirit revealed truths with Spirit-revealed words. Someone living on an entirely human level rejects the revelations of God's Spirit, for they make no sense to him. He can't understand the revelations of the Spirit because they are only discovered by the illumination of the Spirit.

Those who live in the Spirit are able to carefully evaluate all things, and they are subject to the scrutiny of no one but God.

For who has ever intimately known the mind of the Lord Yahweh well enough to become his counselor? Christ has, and we possess Christ's perceptions."

Practically what this means is that, if you are walking or living in the Spirit then your thoughts are an impartation from God's mind. This makes daydreaming critical because it creates a platform for thought transfer from God's mind to your mind.

Daydreaming becomes an unfiltered spontaneous flow of thoughts and revelation from God's Spirit and mind to your spirit and mind. This is a divine uplink for a super download. This is the same as the Hebrew Bible concept known as **"Naba"**, pronounced **"Naw-baw."** Which means to prophesy, speak or make predictions under the inspiration of the Spirit of God. If God can speak through night-dreams, why can't he speak through daydreams?

Daydreaming is a gateway to imagination; this is very important because God is inviting you to think and imagine big. **God's ability to work in you and through you is only hampered by your imagination.**

"Never doubt God's mighty power to work in you and accomplish all this. He will achieve infinitely more than your greatest request, your most unbelievable dream, and exceed your wildest imagination! He will outdo them all, for his miraculous power constantly energizes you." Ephesians 3:20 TPT

2. REPUTATION

It cannot be over-emphasized that, ***"A beautiful reputation is more to be desired than great riches, and to be esteemed by others is more honorable than to own immense investments."*** Proverbs 22:1 TPT. Ecclesiastes 7:1 NLT says that, ***"A good reputation is more valuable than costly perfume."***

Your reputation is one of your greatest assets. It is the product equivalent to branding. The better and more reputable the brand, the more market command it has. Branding is the difference between a $50 and a $500 pair of shoes, both pairs of shoes may have the same production cost and quality from a factory in China. The $500 pair of shoes is marketed to high society as a superior brand though there may not be any real difference to the $50 pair.

Your reputation impacts how people perceive you, your product and services. These perceptions influence how you are branded and your marketability. Protect your reputation the same way you would protect your confidential documents. **It takes a long time to establish a good name, but it doesn't take that much to ruin it.**

Surround yourself with people who will add value to your brand rather than drag it through the mud. How you brand yourself will determine your market value and share. Someone gets paid $5,000 to make an appearance and speech. Someone else will be paid $200,000 for the same speech and appearance at the same place. **Reputation is the most undervalued asset people have. It should be kept under lock and key!**

3. PEOPLE-SKILLS

If your **"Network is your Net worth"**, then I would greatly encourage you to **"Increase your connectedness."** Look at it this way, what if you called in a favor from all your Facebook friends and they each agreed to deposit $10 into your bank account. How much money would you have and how would that significantly change your life? For many of us our outstanding bills will be paid. Though $10 from one person may do very little to change your circumstance, but your collective network will.

Here is an extract from the previous Chapter; *"If success is a symphony, then developing relationship skills is a must. Interpersonal skills are an art which can be learnt by anyone. Make an effort to relate and connect with people. Don't be one of those people who sit in a corner because nobody is talking to them. You never know which conversation will lead to an open door of opportunity. You may identify as, "not a people person", this is a lie, there is nothing like "a people person"* ***there is only loving people!*** *All you must do is take interest in the person in front of you.*

Of course, there are extroverts and introverts, but what does that have to do with loving? In fact, being an introvert can be an advantage because you can listen more, observe and see more. This will give you an edge to connect with people on a deeper level than the mundane superficial interactions."

Many times, in life and business it's not about what you know but *who* you know. A little favor with people will take you a long way. Jesus is the most influential and successful person who ever graced this earth. Would you like to know the key to his success? Here it is, ***"As Jesus grew, so did his wisdom and maturity. The favor of men increased upon his life, for he was loved greatly by God."*** Luke 2:52 TPT. Favor with people will open doors for you that skill, talent or education can't. Favor opened the prison doors for Joseph to become second in command over all Egypt. Favor shut the mouths of lions in the den and elevated Daniel to a position of deputy to Darius. It's called **"human resource"** for a good reason! **People in your life have great and irreplaceable value.** Take care of your relationships and they will take care of you.

Whichever kind of relationship, whether family, friends, employer or employee relationship. **Place great value on it and people will be willing to go an extra mile for you.**

Good people skills foster a productive environment. Where there is love, a wish is a command. ***"David remarked longingly to his men, "Oh, how I would love some of that good water from the well by the gate in Bethlehem."***

So the Three broke through the Philistine lines, drew some water from the well by the gate in Bethlehem, and brought it back to David.

But he refused to drink it. Instead, he poured it out as an offering to the Lord.

"The Lord forbid that I should drink this!" he exclaimed. "This water is as precious as the blood of these men who risked their lives to bring it to me."

So David did not drink it. These are examples of the exploits of the Three." 2 Samuel 23:15-17 NLT

4. CREDIT SCORE

As you embark on your prosperity and wealth-creation journey, sooner or later you will need a capital injection. There are several ways to fund your business venture. You could borrow money from family and friends, seek partnerships, utilize crowdfunding platforms, approach private investors or get a bank loan. Regardless of your funding source, you will have a higher chance of procuring funds if your prospective lender has got a high level of confidence in your ability to make repayments.

Lending institutions have a method of determining this level of confidence in your capacity to make repayments. It's called a credit score or rating. Your credit score is a financial report based on your credit history with current and previous lenders or financial services. In many countries credit scoring is generally an accepted method of assessing your credit worthiness. This Credit score is used to determine whether your credit application should be approved or not. Your credit score can also be used to set your credit limits on credit or store cards.

Most people don't realize how important their credit score is until it is too late. Don't default on your bills. If you can't make the payment negotiate with your lender or provider. Most lenders and service providers are happy for you to make a payment plan or arrangement without resulting into a black mark on your credit score.

To increase your chances for success, check your credit score before applying for a loan. Rectify any negative remarks on your report. This could also be a good way to check if someone else has stolen your identity and is using it to obtain loans.

Consider your credit score as an asset because without it, you will find it extremely difficult to source funding for your business and wealth creation ventures.

Five Ways To IMPROVE Your Credit Score

1. Keep your credit report in order. Maintaining a good credit score will allow you to apply for credit cards and loans with confidence.

2. Have an active credit account.

3. Pay your bills on time.
4. Avoid negative listings at all costs.
5. Avoid too many hard credit enquiries.

Chapter Seventeen

Establishing Intergenerational Wealth

GOD introduced himself to Moses in Exodus 3:6 NLT as an intergenerational God. ***"I am the God of your father –the God of Abraham, the God of Isaac, and the God of Jacob." When Moses heard this, he covered his face because he was afraid to look at God."*** He is interested in your past, present and future. God's desire is to establish his testimony in your life to a thousand generations.

"Understand, therefore, that the Lord your God is indeed God. He is the faithful God who keeps his

covenant for a thousand generations and lavishes his unfailing love on those who love him and obey his commands." Deuteronomy 7:9 NLT. God's intention is not for any of us to be just a fly-by-night blimp in the grand scheme of things. Your life was designed to produce and establish a dynasty.

When I use the word, **"DYNASTY"** two things come mind. The first thing is *a sphere of influence*. ***"The heavens belong to the Lord, but he has given the earth to all humanity."*** Psalm 115:16 NLT. This scripture is an echo of Genesis 1:28 NLT which says, **"Then God blessed them and said, *"Be fruitful and multiply. Fill the earth and govern it. Reign over the fish in the sea, the birds in the sky, and all the animals that scurry along the ground."***

God has put you in charge of the earth. Leaving the exercise of power, influence and possession of the wealth and resources of the earth to other people is irresponsible and bad stewardship. Find your niche in which you can exercise your God given dominion. God has got such a very high opinion of you that leaves angels puzzled.

"What is mankind that you are mindful of them, human beings that you care for them?

You have made them a little lower than the angels and crowned them with glory and honor.

You made them rulers over the works of your hands; you put everything under their feet:" Psalm 8:4-8 NIV

The second aspect of the word **"DYNASTY"** is *succession*. This is when wealth and spheres of influence are passed on from one generation to another. Just as well that the Kingdom of God is not a democracy, otherwise God would have been voted out when some angels rebelled. This is reassuring that your God given mandate can't be taken away from you unless you choose to give it away.

The point is that your dynasty is meant to have heirs and your heirs are meant to have a dynasty. One thing without the other is an incomplete equation. Abram figured this out, look at this passage. ***"Some time later, the Lord spoke to Abram in a vision and said to him, "Do not be afraid, Abram, for I will protect you, and your reward will be great.***

But Abram replied, "O Sovereign Lord, what good are all your blessings when I don't even have a son? Since you've given me no children, Eliezer of Damascus, a servant in my household, will inherit all my wealth.

You have given me no descendants of my own, so one of my servants will be my heir."

Then the Lord said to him, "No, your servant will not be your heir, for you will have a son of your own who will be your heir." Genesis 15:1-4 NLT

Abram had wealth without an heir. Most of us have heirs without wealth but here is God's opinion on the subject, ***"The benevolent man leaves an inheritance that endures to his children's children, but the wealth of the wicked is treasured up for the righteous."*** Psalm 13:22 TPT. A benevolent man is a kind, caring, compassionate and generous person.

THREE BATTLES

My intention here is to provoke someone into action. If you are feeling provoked, then it is time to go to battle. I call this a battle of three fights. **You were born to have dominion, it's time you fought for your mountain.**

Put your faith into action and see the promises and faithfulness of God manifest in your life.

I have always been inspired by a man called Jabez. He came to realize that there should be more to life than just pain and scraping by. He decided he wasn't content with making do and living day by day. Mr. Jabez determined to do something and turn his life around. I guess what inspires me is that his course of action is something we can all do! It is within the capacity of every person. He prayed! He asked God to intervene in his life. If you don't like where you are financially in your life, start with prayer.

"Jabez was more honorable than his brothers. His mother had named him Jabez, saying, "I gave birth to him in pain." Jabez cried out to the God of Israel, "Oh, that you would bless me and enlarge my territory! Let your hand be with me and keep me from harm so that I will be free from pain." And God granted his request." 1 Chronicles 4:9-10 NIV

The name Jabez means pain. His whole life was characterized by pain and hardship and suffering. The Bible says Jabez was an honorable man, yet his life was full of misery. How can someone be honorable and miserable at the same time? There is a lesson I want you to learn here. The mother of Jabez suffered a lot of pain during delivery due to birthing complications. As a result, she named her baby boy pain or Jabez if you will. By naming her child, she prophesied and spoke a destiny of pain, misery and poverty. As the boy grew his name became a self-fulfilling prophecy. What his mother spoke over him is exactly what he became. Jabez's life would have been characterized by stagnation, sickness and disease, financial hardship, lack of breakthrough and void of prosperity. He would work very hard for very little or no return at all. No matter what he did he could never get ahead as though there was a hidden force undermining his efforts. **Jabez was suffering because of the power of spoken words.**

Proverbs 18:21 TPT says this, ***"Your words are so powerful that they will kill or give life, and the talkative person will reap the consequences."***

When you speak life and hope, you come into agreement with the Spirit of God and release life and blessings.

When you speak hopelessness and words which are not life-giving, you come into agreement with an evil spirit and release a curse. This was the case for Jabez when his mother released curses instead of blessing over his life.

I am writing this book to help you to understand that *wealth is a blessing from God and prosperity is a fruit of the Spirit.* Poverty is a curse from the devil, it's got no business in your life and family. Suffering is a demonic assignment to rob you of the joy of walking with God. I am saying this to bring your attention to what kind of words have been spoken over you? These spoken words maybe responsible for your stagnation and struggles in life.

The second aspect is what kind of words have you been speaking over people in your life? You have to understand that whenever you speak, you are either invoking the Spirit of God or demons into action to act on your words. This is why you have to learn to guard your tongue. Words are spirit, ***"The Spirit alone gives eternal life. Human effort***

accomplishes nothing. And the very words I have spoken to you are spirit and life." John 6:63 NLT

CREATING A SUCCESSFUL DYNASTY

To create a successful dynasty, start speaking with hope and life into your future and that of your children. Come into agreement with the Spirit of God. Don't do what Jabez's Father did! Yes, you read it right. I said *Father* not Mother. Give the woman a break! She had just been through a terrible ordeal. She projected her ordeal on the life of a child and Daddy remained silent.

There is thus another lesson to be learned here: *indifference is an enemy to progress, fruitfulness and success.* Another Father in an exact similar situation spoke up and reshaped the future and destiny of a newly born son.

"Leaving Bethel, Jacob and his clan moved on toward Ephrath. But Rachel went into labor while they were still some distance away. Her labor pains were intense. After a very hard delivery, the midwife finally exclaimed, "Don't be afraid–you have another son!"

Rachel was about to die, but with her last breath she named the baby Ben-oni (which means "son of my sorrow").

The baby's father, however, called him Benjamin (which means "son of my right hand")." Genesis 35:16-18 NLT

With one-word Jacob *spared* his son from a life of pain like Jabez. He spoke words that gave rise to a dynasty of formidable warriors among the twelve tribes of Israel. ***"Benjamin is a ravenous wolf, devouring his enemies in the morning and dividing his plunder in the evening."*** Genesis 49:27 NLT.

For some people in order to embark on the road to prosperity, they might need to change their *confession*. Others may have to change their *name*. **When your confession doesn't line up with your destiny, it's time for something to change.** There is a lot of evidence in the Bible where God changed the names of people in order to bring them into alignment with their *purpose, destiny and calling*. Abram was renamed Abraham. He changed Sarai to Sarah, Jacob to Israel, Cephas to Peter, Saul to Paul and so on. Perhaps I could also add myself to this list, He renamed me Victor Isaacs. You can read more about this in my other book, *'Adopted by Abba'*.

TAKE THE MOUNTAIN

We are all carrying God's promises on our lives. The difference is that some people pursue their dreams and promises while others burry their heads in the sand.

The sure thing is 2 Corinthians 1:20 NLT ***"For all of God's promises have been fulfilled in Christ with a resounding "Yes!" And through Christ, our "Amen" (which means "Yes") ascends to God for his glory."*** Some of us have been promised a mountain occupied by giants. You could feel intimidated and walk away from your promise or trust God and face the giants. This is what Caleb decided to do. He recognized that while the giants occupying his promised mountain were imposing and valiant in battle, the God who promised him the mountain was faithful and mighty in battle: ***"A delegation from the tribe of Judah, led by Caleb son of Jephunneh the Kenizzite, came to Joshua at Gilgal. Caleb said to Joshua, "Remember what***

the Lord said to Moses, the man of God, about you and me when we were at Kadesh-barnea.

I was forty years old when Moses, the servant of the Lord, sent me from Kadesh-barnea to explore the land of Canaan. I returned and gave an honest report, but my brothers who went with me frightened the people from entering the Promised Land.

For my part, I wholeheartedly followed the Lord my God. So that day Moses solemnly promised me, 'The land of Canaan on which you were just walking will be your grant of land and that of your descendants forever, because you wholeheartedly followed the Lord my God.'

"Now, as you can see, the Lord has kept me alive and well as he promised for all these forty-five years since Moses made this promise—even while Israel wandered in the wilderness.

Today I am eighty-five years old. I am as strong now as I was when Moses sent me on that journey, and I can still travel and fight as well as I could then.

So give me the hill country that the Lord promised me. You will remember that as scouts we found the descendants of Anak living there in great, walled towns.

But if the Lord is with me, I will drive them out of the land, just as the Lord said." So Joshua blessed Caleb son of Jephunneh and gave Hebron to him as his portion of land. Hebron still belongs to the descendants of Caleb son of Jephunneh the Kenizzite because he wholeheartedly followed the Lord, the God of Israel." Joshua 14:6-14 NLT

However, the thing that amazes me most is, why would an 85-year-old man be wanting to fight to possess a mountain? Most people at his age are either retired or dead! I scratched my head for answers until the Wonderful Counsellor gave me some understanding.

You see, *whatever battles you avoid fighting, your children will have to fight them!* Whatever battles you fight and win are battles your children will never have to fight.

THREE BATTLES OF LIFE

From this study I concluded that there are three battles in life: First, Yesterday's Battle. Second, Today's Battle. Third, Tomorrow's Battle.

1. Yesterday's Battle: HERITAGE

While every battle you can ever fight is unpleasant, fighting yesterday's battles is the most unfortunate. Sadly, I have to say that most people spend the bulk of their lives fighting this battle. This is the battle where we are constantly dealing with the past. We are either trying to resolve or are paying for our past mistakes. **All the resources are committed to addressing the past without any capital left to lay a foundation for the present and the future.** "This is the classic definition of not getting ahead." Why? Because all our future earnings don't belong to our present. This is why the adversary loves it when we are in bad debts.

This is a battle where we find ourselves drowning in generational issues and curses. Have you heard statements like, "This disease is in my family, Grandpa died from it, Dad has it, I have it, I am afraid my kids will have it!" **If it's a pattern that**

keeps on reoccurring in your life and family, whether it is health, finances or just chronic struggling, maybe you are fighting a generational battle!

In yesterday's battle you are fighting for a heritage. ***None of us were meant to be fighting for our inheritance.*** This is something that is meant to be handed down to us as a birthright. This is what happens when Father's pawn the future! It's shocking the number of retired people I see driving around in recreational vehicles, these vehicles have stickers on them which say, "I am spending my children's inheritance." Probably they don't really mean that! But this is the kind of thinking and attitude which disadvantages their offspring. Instead of this new generation establishing their lives on their Father's success and prosperity, they are left struggling to pay off their Father's debts and funeral expenses. This should never be!

Sometimes yesterday's battle is about setting the record right. I find this account in the book of Numbers 27 very fascinating; ***"One day a petition was presented by the daughters of Zelophehad– Mahlah, Noah, Hoglah, Milcah, and Tirzah.***

Their father, Zelophehad, was a descendant of Hepher son of Gilead, son of Makir, son of Manasseh, son of Joseph.

These women stood before Moses, Eleazar the priest, the tribal leaders, and the entire community at the entrance of the Tabernacle.

"Our father died in the wilderness," they said. "He was not among Korah's followers, who rebelled against the Lord; he died because of his own sin. But he had no sons. Why should the name of our father disappear from his clan just because he had no sons? Give us property along with the rest of our relatives."

So Moses brought their case before the Lord. And the Lord replied to Moses, "The claim of the daughters of Zelophehad is legitimate. You must give them a grant of land along with their father's relatives. Assign them the property that would have been given to their father.

"And give the following instructions to the people of Israel: If a man dies and has no son, then give his inheritance to his daughters.

And if he has no daughter either, transfer his inheritance to his brothers. If he has no brothers, give his inheritance to his father's brothers. But if his father has no brothers, give his inheritance to the nearest relative in his clan.

This is a legal requirement for the people of Israel, just as the Lord commanded Moses." Numbers 27:1-11 NLT

Not only did these ladies reach out to the past and drag their inheritance into the present, they also created a precedence which governs and influences modern inheritance laws. They didn't just fight for themselves, they also fought for all the daughters yet to be born daughters.

Yesterday's Fight - Brings us into our inheritance and rewrites the wrong.

Don't be bullied into giving up your birthright! This is your position and portion of sonship. ***The past and pain must not prevent you from walking into your destiny.***

Forgive the past and look forward to the future. Offence and unresolved heart issues can block you from receiving things you want the most. Rest in God. Striving is success rooted in hard work on the other hand, rest is success rooted in relationships.

"Everything we could ever need for life and complete devotion to God has already been deposited in us by his divine power.

For all this was lavished upon us through the rich experience of knowing him who has called us by name and invited us to come to him through a glorious manifestation of his goodness.

As a result of this, he has given you magnificent promises that are beyond all price, so that through the power of these tremendous promises you can experience partnership with the divine nature, by which you have escaped the corrupt desires that are of the world." 2 Peter 1:3-4 TPT

2. Today's Battle - LEGEND

This is the part of the battle Jabez fought. His first battle was to rectify his yesterday, breaking the curse over his life pronounced over him at birth. His second battle was today's battle. He contended for God to bless him and increase his influence. He was no longer content living life in a narrow place.

Deep inside his heart he knew he was born for something much more. He had to expand his dwelling, Jabez was not asking God for a house extension. He was asking for an increase of his estate, he wanted more land, livestock, workers and wealth. He wanted more power and influence in his community. He wanted to matter and make difference.

Today's battle is about increasing your wealth and influence. **Establishing an empire in the area of your gifting and creating a dynasty.** It's about pursuing God's purposes for your life in your generation. It's about going after your dreams and fulfilling your destiny. This is a battle because the enemy is not going to hand it to you on a silver plate. You will have to fight discouragement, failure and the fear of failure, criticism and everything else the enemy, friends and relatives will throw at you. **You may have to draw a line in the sand that all**

generational issues and entanglements end with you and go no further.

I see this kind of fight in King David, he fought and increased the power and influence of Israel. Israel had not enjoyed such prestige since the days of Moses and Joshua. He regained the honor of Israel as a nation whose God was El-Shaddai. His enemies gave him a wide berth. **The amazing thing about establishing yourself is that you also secure the future for your offspring.** This is what I refer to as fighting tomorrow's battle. We go a little bit more into this in the next topic.

FIGHT TO DEFEND YOUR INHERITANCE

Another aspect of Today's battle is that you may need to fight to defend your interests and protect your empire and dynasty. You may have to fight to keep your inheritance. This is what Naboth had to do in 1 Kings 21:1-3 NLT ***"Now there was a man named Naboth, from Jezreel, who owned a vineyard in Jezreel beside the palace of King Ahab of Samaria.***

One day Ahab said to Naboth, "Since your vineyard is so convenient to my palace, I would like to buy it to use as a vegetable garden. I will give you a better vineyard in exchange, or if you prefer, I will pay you for it."

But Naboth replied, "The Lord forbid that I should give you the inheritance that was passed down by my ancestors."

Unlike Esau who sold his birth right for a meal, Naboth refused to sell his inheritance even if it meant losing his very life. The enemy is wicked, he will do anything and throw everything at you in order to undermine your position and capacity to be who you were born to be. He will turn your inheritance into a vegetable garden if you let him. ***"Enlarge your house; build an addition. Spread out your home and spare no expense! For you will soon be bursting at the seams. Your descendants will occupy other nations and resettle the ruined cities.***

Fear not; you will no longer live in shame. Don't be afraid; there is no more disgrace for you. You will no longer remember the shame of your

youth and the sorrows of widowhood." Isaiah 54:21-4 NLT

What the scripture above offers is a pretty good accomplishment, the man has achieved great influence and established himself and his dynasty. He gained much wealth and power. For most people this would be a great place to retire but don't tell that to Caleb. He had to reach for the future and fight Tomorrow's battles as well. THIS IS ABOUT EXPERIENCING THE FULFILMENT OF GOD'S PROMISES IN YOUR LIFE.

3. Tomorrow's Battle - LEGACY

As we look past our natural lives into the future, we establish future generations for success and victory. **Long after we are gone, our actions will echo and reverberate through a test of time and influence future generations.** This becomes our legacy, not only what we leave behind but also what we are remembered by.

What does the future of your children look like because of your actions today? How would future generations know you ever existed? This is your legacy when your present achievements are handed down to your offspring. **This is when your legend becomes your legacy and your legacy becomes your children's inheritance.** This could be money, property or title.

Now this brings me back to Caleb. **At the age of 85 years old, Caleb was challenging to go to battle over the mountain he was promised 40 years earlier on.** He could have said to his offspring, "Look here kids, over there is that mountain occupied by the giants I promised would be your inheritance. I am now retiring; God bless you and good luck with the giants!" Not Mr Caleb, He fought against the giants for the mountain to ensure that his descendants never have to fight. The battle you fight and win are battles your children will never have to fight. The battles you avoid will place a noose around your children's necks.

King David fought all the enemies of Israel, his reign as king was from one fight to another fight. By the time Solomon his son became King, there were no more battles and enemies to be fought. Hence the reign of Solomon was of peace and prosperity. His son never had to work a day in his life because his father's legacy left him with great wealth and influence. **Solomon exceeded because he was building on the foundations of the success and achievements of his father David.** This is how every child was meant to build their lives, not from ground up but from their father's legacy onwards. The next generation can be above and beyond because they were nestled in the lifestyle above and not below! Because your ceiling is their floor.

Tomorrow's Battle secures peace and prosperity for future generations. What you do today can shape the tomorrow for future generations. **Begin to enlarge the tent of your dwelling, increase your influence, building an empire for your children to inherit.** Be a superhero and fight your children's battles like Caleb so that you children won't have to fight. Sure, they will have their own challenges, but your legacy should not be one of them! **Go get that mountain!**

Chapter Eighteen

Rewriting Your Story

THE fact is that most of us aren't born into a trust fund. This unfortunately means we may have to build our lives from the ground up. The good news is that although it's hard, by working *smart* it is do-able. I place emphasis on working smart over working hard because most people work very hard but still live from hand-to-mouth.

I believe that with the *right attitude, information or education and will power anyone can rewrite their story and reach for the stars!* May I also emphasize right education because educational institutions all over the world are designed to produce very good competent workers and not necessarily wealthy people. This explains why most of us have a job but are not particularly successful. This is because our education prepared us for work but not for wealth and prosperity. Nothing wrong with having a job, I will discuss this further in the next chapter.

Prosperity is not luck-of-the-draw, it is strategic thinking, planning, education and embracing God's call on your life. What does God's call on your life have to do with prosperity? **Your provision is often connected to your vision.** A vision is a desire which God puts on your heart. God is obligated to provide for what He has called you to do. When God calls you, He will lead you. Where He leads you, He will provide for you! This is what Matthew 6:33-34 is all about: ***"So above all, constantly chase after the realm of God's kingdom and the righteousness that proceeds from him. Then all these less important things will be given to you abundantly.***

Refuse to worry about tomorrow, but deal with each challenge that comes your way, one day at a time. Tomorrow will take care of itself." TPT

Your vision is your provision. Vision is cardinal to unlocking destiny, purpose, favor, promises and blessings. Vision keeps you in check with where you are in relationship to where you ought to be! Vision is a benchmark which helps us track our progress, it helps us to know which areas of our lives we are doing exceptionally well and the areas we need to pull up our socks. Vision keeps us centered while ambition keeps us motivated.

The sad truth though is that there is very little vision and ambition among God's people. Many people get through life like driftwood downstream. Without vision your life doesn't have a rallying point. You can't master your internal resources to accomplish God's purpose on your life. You need a vision in order to prosper because it provides you with a road map to success for your life. Consider the scripture: ***"When there is no clear prophetic vision, People quickly wander astray. But when you follow the revelation of the Word, Heaven's bliss fills your soul."*** Proverbs 29:18 TPT.

This brings me to 1 Thessalonians 5:19-24 TPT, ***"Never restrain or put out the fire of the Holy Spirit. And don't be one who scorns prophecies but be faithful to examine them by putting them to the test, and afterward hold tightly to what has proven to be right. Avoid every appearance of evil.***

Now, may the God of peace and harmony set you apart, making you completely holy. And may your entire being–spirit, soul, and body–be kept completely flawless in the appearing of our Lord Jesus, the Anointed One. The one who calls you by name is trustworthy and will thoroughly complete his work in you."

Rewriting the story of your life becomes easy and a great joy when you tap into the heavenly blueprints of God's destiny and purpose. It just becomes a case of refocusing and repositioning. **It's about realigning your life with God's calling.** Without stating the obvious, when I talk about rewriting the story of one's life it can be assumed that one's life is off course. In the previous chapter we dealt with generational wealth and challenges. These are some of the issues which could either give you an advantageous edge or a handicap. These could be spiritually motivated or cultural mindsets that can work for you or against you.

I come from a culture where parents believe their children to be their insurance, pension and retirement plan. Well and good, but this leaves the child without an inheritance. Most of the children's resources are committed to taking care of the past instead of establishing the future. This can be argued both sides, in most cultures' children have an obligation to take care of their elderly parents. Biblically parents have a duty to establish an inheritance for their children: ***"The benevolent man leaves an inheritance that endures to his children's children, but the wealth of the wicked is treasured up for the righteous."*** ~ Proverbs 13:22 TPT

Cultural beliefs and mindsets leave me without an inheritance. This means that I will have to fight every inch of the way for every inch of ground I take. Nothing is given, everything has to be fought for.

Not being able to build your life on the success and achievements of your parents can be a disadvantage particularly if life was a race.

The good news is that it is not. If it were, you only have to race against yourself. I have written this book, to encourage someone who feels that life has not dealt them with a good hand. **You may not have been privileged to stand on the shoulders of a giant, but you can be the giant on whose shoulder's others can stand.** You can create the opportunities for other people you wished you had. We all can be for someone what we hoped someone could have been for us.

WHO IS YOUR SOURCE?

As a young boy growing up in Africa, I was constantly told that water does not rise past its source. This was one way of saying, "accept your lot in life, if you are poor, there is nothing you can do about it!" It's a slavery mindset where everybody had to embrace their station and could never aspire for more.

There may be some truth that water can never rise past its source. If your family is your source then you are in trouble but if you recognize Jesus as your source, then you have hope beyond measure!

I believe that every curse can be broken, and every story can be rewritten! What is your story?

Anybody can change their "stars". If your station is a curse, thank God for the cross and the finished work of Jesus. Every curse can be broken! ***The knowledge and understanding that it is God who gives us the strength to acquire wealth is the greatest equalizer for me.*** Believing and embracing the principles and God perspective for prosperity with regards to His purpose over my life made me believe to reach for the stars. I believe in what I have been sharing with you in this book. It's working wonders for me; I am convinced it will do the same for you if you believe.

WHERE TO START

Start consuming the content of this book and make it your personal truth. Embrace God's truth and apply His principles to your life. If you have nothing, you may have to start from somewhere. Most of the time a job is a good place to start from. The problem is that most people with a job get stuck in a rat-race. If you are stuck in a rat-race, your life is like a hamster on a wheel. **Nothing will change until you *interrupt* the cycle.** You must choose to do something differently. Otherwise you will be running the same routine for the next 30 years. Remember the old saying, **"if you do what you have always done then you get what you always got."**

INTERRUPTING THE CYCLE

Any cycle has a particular beat and rhythm. It is perpetuated by consistent follow through and routine. Consistent actions have got consistent results and outcomes. **In order to obtain a different result, you *must risk taking a different set of actions.***

If you are living hand-to-mouth, what would happen if you skipped a couple of meals and used the money to attend a budgeting course or an investing workshop? What if you decided not to go out for coffee, drinks, eat out, cancelled all your unnecessary subscriptions and commitments for one month? How much of your time and resources would be made available to better and improve your position? What if you read a book instead of watching Television, connected with real people in the real world and not social media? What if you took an investment course instead of a holiday or turned in early to sleep instead of going to that party?

Sometimes life is a series of little choices and decisions which make a huge difference in success and stagnation. People who exercise self-discipline and sacrifice are most often successful and prosperous than not. When my children are asking to have or do things which their friends have or are doing, I would ask them the "question": **"What would you prefer, have fun now and then sweat for the rest of your life or sweat now and then have fun for the rest of your life?"**

The point is that too often we sacrifice the future for a fleeting moment of pleasure. In our microwave culture people are always thinking about now and never spare a moment to think about tomorrow. ***If we could learn to sacrifice today for the sake of a better tomorrow, we will have a brighter future!***

When finances are tight it's difficult to invest and break that cycle of pay-cheque-to-pay-cheque.

Here is my how to break the cycle secret: *always pay your bills starting by paying the little guy first.* The little guy needs the money just like you do. Then negotiate to make a flexible payment arrangement with the big guys. I discovered that the big guys don't need my $500 to stay afloat and are usually happy for me to enter into a payment arrangement. I can pay them the $500 over the next couple of months if I sacrifice eating out and some socializing. By doing this I have interrupted my cycle so I can afford to invest $500 in myself. The key is to put that $500 towards something which will bring a return and improve your financial position. I have used $500 as an example, depending on your financial capacity this could be more or less.

For example, someone could interrupt their cycle and spend $350 to attend a two-day real-estate course. After the two-day course they get a second part time job as a sales agent and sell a house for a $15,000 commission! Quite a substantial return for the investment and I don't suppose this person would have any trouble making the bill payment.

This is just one of the many examples and this is not beyond the realm of possibilities. People who invested $100 in Bitcoin ten years ago are millionaires today! Like I said earlier in this book, the only limitation is your imagination. You can complain about your circumstances or do something about it. The choice is yours.

"Brilliant ideas pay off and bring you prosperity, but making hasty, impatient decisions will only lead to financial loss." Proverbs 21:5 TPT

SAVING FOR A RAINY DAY

Saving money is not just a good idea, it's a God idea. The ability to save money marks the difference between consumers and investors, the poor and the prosperous.

The reason why there are so many financially challenged people than financially thriving people is that most of the time it comes down to spending habits.

Financially there are three kinds of people. The first and most common kind of people are *spenders or consumers*. The second group of people are those described in the parable of the talents in Matthew 25:18, they dig a hole and *bury their money*. Then there those who *invest*, these are the ones who become wealthy and prosperous! Listen to this ancient wisdom, ***"The wise have wealth and luxury, but fools spend whatever they get."*** Proverbs 21:20 NLT

Saving is only the first step to prosperity. **If saving is all we ever do, then we are not any different from the fool in Matthew 25:18.** I have heard a lot of people say that they are saving some money for a rainy day. Saving is a good start but saving for a rainy day should never be the motivation or the goal. I don't know about you, but where I come from it's always raining! The problem is that it always seems to be pouring heavy rain every other day. This means that the rainy-day savers are always spending their savings! It kind of defeats the purpose doesn't it?

Consequently, most people are caught up in a loop: Earn-Save-Rain-Spend-Broke = Earn-Save-Rain-Spend-Broke, and so it goes on and on.

The cycle will continue until you decide to interrupt the sequence.

Sometimes I feel overwhelmed by the number of requests for financial help I receive from extended family, friends, pastors, missionaries, churches and ministries. I realized that responding to people's need can be a full-time job which never ends.

I read about one of God's Generals, Dr John G Lake while at the height of his ministry healing the sick and feeding the hungry, his own wife died of neglect and starvation! The hard lesson here is that we can be too engrossed in everything else and miss the things which really matter. Sometimes it's like they say on the airplane, before you attempt to assist someone else, please secure your own oxygen mask first. If you pass out, then you won't be of any help to anybody.

RECOGNISE YOUR MOMENT

Jesus once had an intense conversation at Simon's house in Bethany. He taught His disciples the value of recognizing what is most important in the moment they were in.

There will always be issues and needs competing for your time and resources. You will need to learn what is known in medical terms as **"Triage"**. This is the word used to assign the degree of urgency to wounds or illnesses to decide the order of treatment of a large number of patients or casualties.

"Meanwhile, Jesus was in Bethany at the home of Simon, a man who had previously had leprosy. While he was eating, a woman came in with a beautiful alabaster jar of expensive perfume made from essence of nard. She broke open the jar and poured the perfume over his head.

Some of those at the table were indignant. "Why waste such expensive perfume?" they asked. "It could have been sold for a year's wages and the money given to the poor!" So they scolded her harshly. But Jesus replied, "Leave her alone. Why criticize her for doing such a good thing to me?

You will always have the poor among you, and you can help them whenever you want to. But you will not always have me. She has done what she could and has anointed my body for burial ahead of time.

I tell you the truth, wherever the Good News is preached throughout the world, this woman's deed will be remembered and discussed." Mark 14:3-9 NLT

The point I am making is that you will always have a rainy day! **If you are going to save some money, be *intentional, strategic and specific.*** Put aside some money for a purpose. You have to understand that the devil uses these rainy days to keep you trapped and caged in poverty. He is the architect of these events and situations are tailored to steal and divert your resources away from increase and breakthrough. When you save up money for a house deposit, the enemy will want you to spend that money at the vet for a cat or dog bill. This is his design to short-circuit your progress. To break or to interrupt that cycle of poverty, you need to be intentional with your saving. **Save up for a seed to plant not for a rainy day.** Like a wise farmer, resist the urge to eat the seed. Eating the seed, no matter how genuine the reason may be only perpetuating poverty.

SALARIES ARE FOR INVESTMENTS

A job is what our educational system prepares us for. We do the best we can in school or university so we can get the best job we can. The higher paying the job we have, the better houses, cars, etc. we can afford or the bigger the loans we can qualify for.

Before we know it, we find ourselves trapped in a superficial life we have created where we must get up every morning to punch in the timecard so we can stay on top of the bills. This reminds me of when I was a small boy in grade school in a science class. I was a bit confused on what was the correct statement, ***"Do we eat in order to live or do we live in order to eat?"*** This confusion is the same for most people when it comes to having a job, do you work in order to live to or do you live in order to work? Either way you are in trouble! If you work in order to live, then you will always need to work to survive. You are like a hamster stuck on a wheel. If you live to work, then you are a slave!

When my son was about 13 years old, he asked me if he could work at his friend's family restaurant. For a 13-year-old having a job was an incredible character developing exercise. It was a good way for him to appreciate the value of earning money and hard work. He was going to work one to two hours wobble-boarding for $5 an hour. That meant $5-$10 in his pocket. This also presented me with an opportunity to teach my son something else beyond hard work! **It is called working smart!**

This is the difference between rich people and poor people. Poor people work hard while rich people work smart! This means that the rich get more money for their time and make more money out of your time.

Smart work 101: for my son to make $5, I had to sacrifice 30 minutes of my productivity. This meant I had to stop working such as writing this book to drop and pick him up from work plus the cost of running my 3L-Turbo Diesel truck and the wear-and-tear on the vehicle. Besides him learning hard work I had to demonstrate the value of time that it actually cost me about $30 for him to make $5. When we don't learn this lesson, we will most likely run the time/reward ratio in our lives at a deficit.

This means that we are doing more work for little return, unlike the rich who do less work for more return. As you can see, this is hardly the formula for success and prosperity. As a worker or employee, your time is a commodity for sale at a fixed rate per hour to an employer. **On the other hand, as an entrepreneur your time is like a seed with a potential for multiple returns.** This is the difference between you working for money or money working for you. Let's pick up on this topic in the next chapter.

Chapter Nineteen

EMPLOYMENT OR ENTREPRENEURSHIP?

IF the point of working is not to just get by but to make a living, to maximize our potential to be the best we can and produce much fruit; I think it's imperative that we re-evaluate *the three most common methods we earn a living or make money: employment, self-employment and entrepreneurship or business.*

We mostly make money by engaging in either one or a combination of these three methods. For most of us we just do what we saw our parents do or we are trained and educated to do without putting much thought into it. I hope this chapter will help you to evaluate and determine the most efficient way to get the most out of your potential, gifting and skills in order to fulfil your mandate. **"The mandate to be fruitful, increase, multiply, rule and have dominion."**

EMPLOYMENT

This is the most common and popular way to earn a living. It has become a way of life. **Educational systems and institutions of higher learning are set up to prepare their graduates for service and employment.** From pre-school, the educational focus is on what **"Job"** you want to have when you grow up.

There is nothing wrong with preparing future employees. **The problem is the "Cookie-cutter educational systems" which create uniformity at the expense of exceptionalism and actually cut out uniqueness.** With that said, let's get into it! What is Employment or who is an Employee?

You are an employee when you are engaged to work or provide service to an employer. Your employer is obliged to take off Income Tax and mandated contributions from your salary or wages before paying them to you. As an employee you are entitled to employment rights such as; sick pay, maternity, adoption and paternity leave. Of course, these payments depend upon local regulations and laws. You also have the right not to be unfairly dismissed or given redundancy pay.

These entitlements are what makes employment very appealing. **They provide a sense of security.** It removes uncertainty by knowing that no matter what happens you are not going to be left hanging. The better the education we have, the better the job we can get with more entitlements and opportunities to move up the ladder into middle and upper management.

SELF-EMPLOYMENT

Self-employment means you do not have a contract of employment with an employer. You provide services to others either once-off or on a regular basis for a fee. You are in business in your own right. You are a sole proprietor; you are responsible for paying your own taxes and other mandated contributions. You don't have employment entitlements as such listed above for employees. You are your own boss. You can decide how much to charge for your work and how much holiday to give yourself. In other words, you are creating a job for yourself ~ if you don't get out of bed, the job is not going to get done and you don't get paid. What if you are sick?

While the thought of being your own boss is awesome, most of us choose to sacrifice our freedom over security. We are trained to approach life with the worst possible scenario in mind. **Fear of the "what if" prevents us from exploring our possibilities and capacity. Caution helps us to approach the unknown carefully, but fear stops us from stepping out altogether**. I am saying this because people confuse caution with fear.

ENTREPRENEURSHIP OR BUSINESS

Businesses come in all shapes and sizes from small, medium to large. In business there is a perception of risk and reward synonym. When things go wrong you loose and when they go your way you win. As a business owner, you own a business and hire employees, contractors, or both.

Many people start as self-employed entrepreneurs and grow into a business over time. Entrepreneurship can help you explore your creativity and potential while utilizing your skills. It gives you a wide avenue to market your skills and gifting instead of just having one customer, "the employer," while retaining the freedom of being your own boss. Unlike the self-employed, you don't have to close shop when you take a holiday because you have employees.

As a business owner, there is no limit on how much money you can make, for as long as your business is performing, and your product or service is in demand. You will make more money and grow bigger and bigger. As an employee, no matter how much money your employer makes, you only take home your contract pay, maybe a bonus. It is not a surprise that wealthy people have businesses and not a job.

INVESTMENTS

Two things most wealthy and rich people have are businesses and investments. I have talked a bit about business. Maybe a little known or less known thought about source of income for most of us is investing.

The idea of working is to make a living, while the idea of investing is to have a living without having to work. **It's the difference between working for money or money working for you.** Modern civilization has proved that money is a very cruel taskmaster to work for. It has enslaved generations and drove countless others to an early grave.

On the other hand, money has also proved be a very reliable servant, it can work harder and longer without ever needing a break, holiday or sick leave.

When you invest, your money will work for you 24/7, 365 days a year. Whether you sleep in, spend the day at the beach or take on a more noble cause to help the needy, your investments will still yield a reward for you. Investing gives you a way out with a secure source of income when you cannot work for whatever reason.

Perhaps take an early retirement so you can focus on things that really matter to you. You can always pass on your investments to your children as an inheritance. What if you could start as an employee, transition into self-employment and later go into Business?

The good news is that regardless of what you do for a living, you can start to invest. There are a lot of opportunities out there. Seek counsel and advice to find the best options for you. **There is never a better excuse for failing to invest for your future.**

DO NOT LIMIT YOURSELF

Having a job is a good start. However, we should challenge ourselves to reach the limits of our capacity and not just to settle for a false sense of security. Let's demand more out of life than what we have been led to believe. We should all have jobs, it's important and necessary for our growth and development. **A job should never be an end in itself, rather a means to an end.**

It's a great injustice to get your entire life, all the creative genius, potential, skills and gifting and commit it to a single employer.

This is often done at the expense of reaching the millions of lives you were born to touch and influence. The seed of greatness within needs room to grow and flourish than the confinements created by the cookie-cutter.

Now imagine this, the employer you are committed to serving as an employee decides how much they think your service, skill and gifting are worth. In this case your potential is considered a raw talent, you will never get paid for it. If you come up with an innovative idea at work, guess what! The Boss owns it. Maybe that explains why you hardly ever meet rich and wealthy workers; you only meet rich and wealthy entrepreneurs.

Entrepreneurs take their skills, gifting and potential to touch and influence the masses or the highest bidder.

Demand for your uniqueness, skills and realized potential puts you in a strong position to negotiate and set your terms and conditions.

Entrepreneurship is the best way to express your ability and stewardship over what God has entrusted to you. God expects more out of you. **You cannot afford to limit your potential by restricting your productivity output.**

The Matrix of Success

The matrix of success is about numbers and increased productivity. **The more people you have queuing for your services, gifting and talent, the higher the value you can place on your services.** This is called demand and supply. If everyone on the market seeking your type of service or product were a pie, then the people coming to you will be your market share. This would also determine your market value.

When your seed of greatness is committed to a single employer, your marketability is restricted and confined to that employer. There is no competition for your brilliance and certainly no bidding competitors fighting over your services, products and abilities. What I am saying is that, *as an employee you only have one customer.*

As an entrepreneur, the sky is the limit. Your earning potential is also limitless.

You are so great and too big to keep your potential contained. You are a wild mustang; you were not born for the fences. **The power, capacity and ability in you needs to be unleashed for the glory of God.** You were born to be a city on the hill for all to see. This is the whole concept of branding. How a product is marketed, will determine how much people are willing to pay for it. The level of excellence in quality and the efficiency of marketing makes a brand. People's perception of a brand determines how much people will be willing to pay.

YOUR JOB IS A SEED

Use your job as a seed to propagate and grow the empire inside of you. I usually like to remind my children about the greatness within them. I will privy you to some of our family conversations. One day my teenage son was offered a job. Full of excitement he came to ask for my blessing to take the job. I appreciated his enthusiasm and willingness to work. Like I said earlier, a job is an important part of our growth and development. It is in a work environment that we are meant to learn interpersonal skills, broaden our experiences and learn some leadership skills. There are things in life you can only learn by doing.

This job for my son was a great opportunity for me teach my son an important life-lesson: *the real value of a job is not to earn money but to learn.* **People who fail to learn at work end up being slaves to the pay-check and employer.** People who learn soon out-grow their job and move on to bigger and better things and perhaps owning their own company or business. **The mistake most people make is that they get a job to earn a living.** This means that for as long as you live, you will always need a job to survive! Some of you might say, "I have a pension, retirement scheme or plan." That's great, but the truth is that for most people the retirement package runs out before they die. The miracle of modern health care is that people live longer and outlast their resources. **Remember, wealth should be intergenerational.**

Your resources are meant to outlast you and then be passed on to your children as their starting point. None of us were meant to live off our jobs.

Think of a job as starter-motor in your car. With the help of other components, it gets your engine running. But it takes several other parts working together in harmony to keep your car moving from point-A to point-B. **The income from your job is seed to sow into wealth creation investments. Look at it as leverage for wealth creation instead of a way of life or a means to survive.** People who fail to grasp this concept are condemned to the life of a hamster treading the spinning wheel. I wanted my son to understand these principles early on in life rather than later. It's much easier to organize your lifestyle in conformity to productivity than to make amendments and correction at a later stage.

THE BIBLE ON INCOME

God has a lot to say about how you spend your money throughout the whole Bible. **This is not a teaching about giving so I will only give you a quick overview.**

I am aware that there is not a subject among most Christians which raises eyebrows and heart attitudes like money, more especially giving.

The truth is that regardless of your theology and doctrine the Biblical principles of finances in both the Old and New Testaments made their adherers both wealthy and prosperous. If you are to prosper, you can't afford to ignore these Biblical financial principles. **Through these principles and practices God transformed a nation of slaves into a great and powerful nation.** This gives me hope for anybody no matter how impoverished they may be. Let's consider this picture; ***"When you reap the harvest of your land, don't reap the corners of your field or gather the gleanings. Leave them for the poor and the foreigners. I am GOD, your God."*** Leviticus 23:22 MSG.

BIBLE MODEL

MODERN MODEL

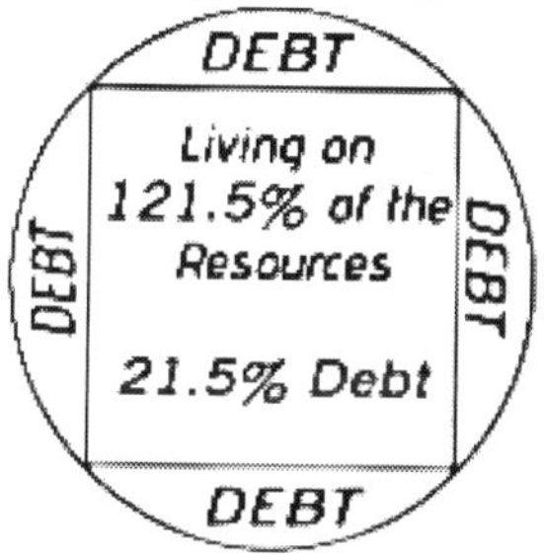

Keep in mind that God is talking here to farmers. Their source of income is the produce from the land which they would trade for silver and gold. This is equivalent to salary or earnings from your job or business. Now look at the picture of what God is asking the people to do: if your field was a square, God is asking you not to harvest the corners. In order to accomplish this, you will have to make a circle within your square. This will look something like the illustrations.

From God's perspective we are only meant to live on 78.5% of our income and resources. Imagine that! *This is possible if you discipline yourself not to borrow money to buy things you can't afford.* **Develop a practice of saving up until you can afford it. This way you will always be ahead and not trying to catch up from behind.**

TITHES / FIRST FRUITS

The whole Bible concept of giving was designed to enrich and not to deprive you of your resources. The Bible talks about three types of Tithes (10% of your income) and at least three types of offerings:

the First-fruits offering, the Sin offering and the Freewill offering. The first fruit offering which was to be given to the Priest, a first fruit of the harvest which is about two-and-a-half percent.

The three tithes were to be given in a sequential rotation. For example, ten-percent of the harvest in year-one was to be taken to the House of God. Another further ten-percent would be given to the giver as savings. This would be exchanged for silver or gold.

Repeat the same process in the second year. In the third year instead of paying the ten-percent to the giver for savings, it would be given to the Levites in the local community to be distributed to the poor. **It might be worth mentioning that the priests were to live on the first fruits offering and not the tithes.** So, what would this look like for you and me today? Glad you asked.

Remember the farmers in the Bible received the income annually hence they paid their tithes and offerings annually. For us today we get paid weekly, fortnightly or monthly. According to your pay frequency, take your first fruits offering from your income, 2.5% percent and give it to your priest, pastor or man of God. Now take 10% of what is left and give it to your church. Still with me? Now take another 10% of what is left and put it into your savings account! Repeat the process with the second pay-check. On the third pay-check, don't pay yourself the ten-percent but give it to the poor or whatever charitable program your church operates.

This approach among Jews meant they were hardly ever in debt because they lived within their resources. In addition, they saved ten-percent of their income while honoring God by giving and God blessed them in turn. **By the time an Israelite died, he had plenty of wealth saved up for his children to inherit.** His children did the same and the wealth grew generation after generation. Imagine if you saved ten-percent of your income from the age of twenty, how much would you have at seventy-years old.

You could do the same with the income from your job or business. If you committed to saving ten-percent in no time at all you will be able to invest in some wealth creation ventures.

Think of the future, don't just live for today. **"If you don't have at least one million dollars in savings and assets like most people, please maintain a life insurance that will cover the needs of your loved ones."** It's hard enough for your family to lose you without leaving them with bills to pay, debts and in poverty.

Chapter Twenty

The Art of Success

I KNOW you have been looking forward to reading this chapter. There is nothing more exciting than mastering the Art of Success.

For those of you with discernment and foresight, you may have noticed that throughout the pages of this book so far, I have laid a trail of gold nuggets. This trail of gold nuggets is not to lead you to one giant gold mine. The idea is to collect all the gold nuggets through the book and gather them into one big treasure vault.

There are no shortcuts to succeeding. But with a little ingenuity, hard work, opportunity and time, there is no telling what you can achieve. The greatest wealth in life is not money but knowledge and understanding. When you look at the 2008 Global Financial Crisis, it's mostly the poor and the middle class who lost their money. The Rich got bonuses and made more money. Here is the thing! **The Rich understand the art and process of creating wealth. This knowledge can never be taken away from them. Wealth and money may be taken away from them but given time, they will soon be back on top because they know the path which leads to the top.**

Poverty is not a lack of resources but the absence of knowledge and understanding. Africa is the richest continent on earth as far as natural resources are concerned. The wealthiest countries in the last two-hundred years were built on the backs of African slaves and resources yet Africans today still live in abject poverty. What is wrong with this picture? Lack of knowledge and understanding! Here is what God has to say about knowledge.

"My people are destroyed from lack of knowledge. Because you have rejected knowledge, I also reject you as my priests; because you have ignored the law of your God, I also will ignore your children." Hosea 4:6 NIV. What is killing people is not poverty but ignorance. If you find a cure for ignorance, then you have found a cure for poverty. I am happy to report that there is a cure for ignorance, it is called knowledge. We are told that, ***"When there is no clear prophetic vision, people quickly wander astray. But when you follow the revelation of the word, heaven's bliss fills your soul."*** Proverbs 29:18 TPT

Proverbs 4:7 gives us an insight into the Art of Success, it says, ***"Wisdom is the most valuable commodity–so buy it! Revelation knowledge is what you need–so invest in it!"*** TPT. Place great value on learning, developing your gift and skills. This is the best investment you can ever make. I cannot emphasis this point enough! The King James Version puts it this way, ***"Wisdom is the principal thing; therefore, get wisdom: and with all thy getting get understanding."*** Proverbs 4:7 KJV.

So, what is the first point in the Art of Success? Knowledge, wisdom and understanding! In moving on, Jesus made an incredible observation about the Kingdom of God. This truth is also very relevant to the Art of Success. Here is what he said, ***"The Kingdom of Heaven is like a treasure that a man discovered hidden in a field. In his excitement, he hid it again and sold everything he owned to get enough money to buy the field."*** Matthew 13:44 NLT.

THE ART OF SUCCESS

From this scripture I would like to make some pertinent remarks with regards to the Art of Success:

1. *The man discovered the treasure in the field.* The treasure did not discover the man. In other words, the man wasn't just sitting around waiting for something to happen. He went out and actively searched for opportunities to change his story. What is my point? Begin to research the possibilities and look for opportunities for your breakthrough.

2. *The treasure was hidden.* It takes patience and discernment to uncover anything of great worth. Don't be in a hurry to make it big otherwise you will miss something important. Take time to evaluate and understand your environment. Proverbs 25:2, ***"It is God's privilege to conceal things and the king's privilege to discover them."*** NLT. This means that real treasures don't come cheap and easy. You have committed to playing the game of hide and seek with God. God conceals a matter, you uncover it. Nature hides the treasures, you discover them. Be an opportunity explorer and venture in places others have only dreamt about.

3. *When the man discovered the hidden treasure, he covered it back again.* He hid the treasure until such a time when he was adequately prepared to purchase the field. He did not broadcast his discovery for everyone to know. This is called wisdom. Most people have lost their opportunities because they spoke too soon to wrong people. Not everybody is interested in your success. **Some people in your life are happy to see you fail and they can't wait to tell you, "I told you so!"** You should not broadcast everything in your life, learn to pick the right time and the right people to talk to. Some people are there to help while others are there to sabotage.

4. *Evidently the man could not afford to buy this field. But that did not deter him from purchasing the field.* This is good news for all of us. Instead of being frustrated and discouraged like most of us are. This man chose to convert his energy into something useful and productive. The man evaluated all the possessions he had; he compared the total value to the value of the treasure he had discovered in the field. I don't suppose it was any surprise to discover that the value of the treasure he found was far greater than the value of everything he owned put together.

Here is the heart of this story, this man did not allow the sentimental value of his possessions to stop him from acquiring great treasure. Sentiment will never put food on your table! Some people are so attached to things that they fail to see the big picture. **The Art of Success is about looking forward not sentiments.** If you are better off with it, hang on to it. If you are better off without it, get rid of it. Don't allow your emotions to cloud your judgement. The man went and sold everything he had and purchased the field with greater treasures. He became wealthy and prosperous because he chose to look forward to the future and not hang on to the past. **The golden old days are just simply that, "OLD!"** What sentiments, be it possessions, relationships and places are preventing you from acquiring great treasures?

5. *Don't be the idiot who sold the field with hidden treasure.* To really appreciate this statement, you have to understand how the treasure got in the field in the first place. Do you remember in the previous chapter I talked about the Jews saving 10% of their harvest? I also mentioned that they would trade that harvest for silver and gold. Well, back then they did not have banks to deposit the silver and gold savings. So, they took clay pots and filled them with such treasures and then buried these clay pots in the field for safety. Talk about a long term deposit!

The problem with this picture is that a Father is dead, and his son has obviously inherited the property. Unfortunately, the financially struggling son has to sell the property just to survive.

Unknown to him, his father had left behind such a great vast wealth of which he had saved up his whole life. In today's money, this would be hundreds of millions of dollars, even a billion. The question is, how come the son didn't know about this treasure? Maybe the father died a sudden death! How come he was the only one who knew where the treasure was buried? Was the son in good standing with his father? Whatever the issue, somebody made an enormous error! **This goes to show that when it comes to the Art of Success, trust, good communication and sound relationships are imperative.**

Take time to share and communicate things that really matter with people who really matter in your life. There are so many people out their suffering because they don't even know that their father or spouse left them a great fortune in investments and life insurances. Take time to understand what you have. I often say to my family, **"if you don't know what something is, don't throw it away!"** Don't suffer because of ignorance. Not knowing is never a better excuse for failing!

THERE IS NO SUBSTITUTE FOR SOWING AND WORKING

Remember God gives seed to the sower. This is his way of providing for you. While God provides the seed, it is your responsibility to sow if you want a harvest. Living by faith is not sitting waiting for the seed to plant itself. Your faith must work together with your actions otherwise your faith is dead.

> ***"My dear brothers and sisters, what good is it if someone claims to have faith but demonstrates no good works to prove it? How could this kind of faith save anyone? For example, if a brother or sister in the faith is poorly clothed and hungry and you leave them saying, "Good-bye.***
>
> ***I hope you stay warm and have plenty to eat," but you don't provide them with a coat or even a cup of soup, what good is your faith? So, then faith that doesn't involve action is phony. But someone might object and say, "One person has faith and another person has works."***

> ***Go ahead then and prove to me that you have faith without works and I will show you faith by my works as proof that I believe."*** James 2:14-18 TPT

> ***"Whoever watches the wind will not plant; whoever looks at the clouds will not reap."*** *Ecclesiastes 11:4* NIV.

The Message translations says it this way,

> ***"Don't sit there watching the wind. Do your own work. Don't stare at the clouds. Get on with your life."*** Ecclesiastes 11:4 MSG.

The Apostle Paul had this to say about working to earn money in 2 Thessalonians 3:10-12 NLT, ***"Even while we were with you, we gave you this command: "Those unwilling to work will not get to eat." Yet we hear that some of you are living idle lives, refusing to work and meddling in other people's business.***

We command such people and urge them in the name of the Lord Jesus Christ to settle down and work to earn their own living."

There are no two ways about it. You don't sow you don't reap! You don't work, you don't eat! Unless you live in a country with a welfare system, you will eat but never realize your full potential.

EARTH'S GOLDEN RULE

> ***"As long as the earth remains, there will be planting and harvest, cold and heat, summer and winter, day and night."*** Genesis 8:22 NLT.

For as long as you are on this side of paradise, plant your seed and you shall have your harvest. Winters come so we can have summer just like difficulties and challenges come so we can have victory.

WRITE THE VISION

When you envision your future, what do you see? What do you hope to achieve or accomplish? Write it down! The first step to becoming what you want to be is to visualize yourself there already. If you can see it in your mind, it's easy to work toward it.

We can't become what we can't see. It's amazing how God throughout the Bible always gave His prophets a word or vision before He could ask them to do something. It was much easier for the prophets to act on something they had seen in a vision even though there was no evidence of it in the natural. I have already talked about the power of imagination. Likewise, vision is key to prosperity and the Art of Success.

Do you remember Proverbs 29:18? ***"When there is no clear prophetic vision, people quickly wander astray. But when you follow the revelation of the word, heaven's bliss fills your soul."*** TPT.

The Lord said to the Prophet Habakkuk, ***"And then God answered: "Write this. Write what you see. Write it out in big block letters so that it can be read on the run."*** Habakkuk 2:2 MSG. It's believed that the cemetery is the richest place on earth. Trillions of dollars of unrealized revenues in potential and ideas are buried without leaving behind a paper trail. Writing down your vision puts your ideas on paper. This will help you to articulate your thoughts in an intelligible way which is easy for you track and communicate.

None of us can succeed on our own. Chapter 15 describes success as symphony. Sooner or later you will need help from other people. Success to procure the necessary investments for your idea to become reality depends on your level of communication.

People will never invest in an idea in your mind, but they are more likely to invest in an idea you put down on paper. IN YOUR MIND it's a thought, on paper it's a Business Plan. Any banker or investor will always ask to see your Business Plan. **Your ideas on paper take you half way to the Art of Success.**

LET'S PUT THIS JIGSAW PUZZLE TOGETHER

Like I said earlier: I have been laying a trail of gold nuggets throughout this book. I understand it can be overwhelming to keep up with. So, let's go over some ideas, thoughts and concepts. It's time to collect the gold nuggets!

MONEY CRAFT

Making money is an act of incredible creativity which comes from God. From our creative processing we can conceptualize solutions to challenges around us. In serving and seeking to add value to people we in turn increase our own value which can be quantified in value returns.

The value return will determine how much people are willing to pay for your services. Service is what we do for others, Value is people's perception of what we do for them. It's a matter of productivity and branding. Value added to your creative processing equals service which means money in your pocket.

The hallmark of making money is embedded in the pursuit of service to people around us. Making money without serving people is called exploitation. **True value is realized when we seek to improve and make the lives of people around us better.** If our goal is to add value to people, then we will serve them with a spirit of excellence. Whenever there is excellence, there is always a high degree of value return.

People want to associate themselves with excellence and are willing to pay more for excellence. **Excellence promotes you, this we find in the life of Daniel.**

Employment

In employment you take your creative processing power and commit it to the service of one customer for a stipulated value return as determined by that single customer. Return on service and productivity is always within the confines of what one customer is willing to pay. There is no benefit of increase in returns as a result of market share expansion. Any increase of revenue and productivity only improves the employers net worth.

Enterprise

In enterprise you take your creative processing power and make it available to everyone. It's called being an entrepreneur. You are committed to serving and adding value to many people rather just one individual or company.

This enables you to cultivate value for your services. This value becomes your branding and it is this branding that determines how much people are willing to pay for your services or products. Any increase in market share or value increases your net worth. This explains why owners of companies, business and corporations get wealthier, but the employees have very little to show after 30 years of dedicated service.

Working for yourself means working for everyone. If people are happy with your services, you will be successful. **The heart of success is not about how much money you can make but about how many people you can reach and help.** This is why wealth creation goes hand in had with God's heart for the welfare of his people. Wealth creation is God's idea. **Wealth creation begins with serving the one in front of you, that will open doors and opportunities to reach and serve more people.** Service rendered to more people means more income or revenue.

BE A BLESSING TO OTHERS

> ***"I've left you an example of how you should serve and take care of those who are weak. For we must always cherish the words of our Lord Jesus, who taught, 'Giving brings a far greater blessing than receiving."*** Acts 20:35 TPT.

A lot of life flows through this verse. Our natural propensity is to focus on ourselves in an attempt to solve our own problems. The issue with this attitude is that if you are busy working on your problem, who is paying for your time?

If you can spend time creating solutions for other people's problems, they will pay you enough to more than just meet your own needs. If you can be an answer to the questions around, you become indispensable and command value. **Our value is in what we offer or give not in what we take or receive.**

People Skills

If making money is about serving people, then you must learn to become a people person. If people like you, they trust you and come to you for services. Deuteronomy 8:18 is the art of serving people. Increase your connectedness and your Network will increase. The size of your Network will determine the size your Net-worth.

PRODUCTIVITY

Productivity means to find a way to serve other people. Making money is a byproduct of services and products rendered to people! The more people we can serve, the more money we can make. This is the concept of mass production. The profit margins are on volume. In high value branding, you create a niche market. The profit margins are on high quality and reputation. Whichever way you look at it, you are either serving the masses of people for $10 each or a select few for a $1000 each.

The Bottom line is, by making money you are serving people, by serving people you are serving God. This is the reason why God wants you to prosper and succeed.

Your success enables you to be a blessing to God's people. The nation of Israel was preserved from perishing as a result of a terrible famine because Joseph had become wealthy, successful and prosperous. **Believe it or not, you have greater value to people when you are successful than when you are poor and broke.** As a matter of fact, God can even do more through you when you are successful! So, here is a list of five things you should have on your way to becoming a success.

Five things you *should* have!

1. A job
2. A business
3. Assets
4. Stocks and bonds
5. Commodities

Remember, most rich people have businesses and investments not a job.

A LITTLE THANKS GOES A LONG WAY

> ***"Let joy be your continual feast. Make your life a prayer. And in the midst of everything be always giving thanks, for this is God's perfect plan for you in Christ Jesus."*** 1Thessalonians 5:16-18 TPT.

A cheerful demeanor helps to maintain optimism even the in darkest times. Gratitude will keep you focused on the bright side in challenges and setbacks. Setbacks are setups for something greater. This is also a way of worshiping and expressing our trust and confidence in God. **Whatever the situation looks like, you can rest assured that God is working out the answer.**

BE WILLING TO TAKE RISKS

You have probably heard the saying, "No pain no gain". Most people will never reach half the potential of their capacity because they are afraid of failure. **The truth is if you have never failed then you have never lived.** We prefer "job security" to "risk taking", the reality is that great success belongs to the brave and daring. **The bigger the risk, the bigger the potential reward.**

Never allow fear to stand in the way of your breakthrough. Don't be one of those people who can see problems in everyone and everything. Be the optimist, see possibilities and find the positive situations. Dig past the dirt and find the gold.

THE MAN WHO COULDN'T READ

I once read on a poster while riding on a ferry about a man who couldn't read. This guy pulled off one of the greatest feats of achievement. Bewildered with wonder and amazement people said to him, "Look here! The sign says that this couldn't be done, how come you were able to do it? The man simply replied, "I didn't know that it couldn't be done because I can't read so I just went and didn't it."

THE WORLD IS LOOKING FOR A TRAILBLAZER

As a trailblazer, you open the possibilities to people. Every milestone you achieve helps others believe that they too can do it.

Ever noticed with every world record there is always a record breaker ensuing in the wings?

Chapter Twenty-One

WHAT DO YOU HAVE?

"In Him we live and move and have our being." If the whole issue of identity and essence of who we are is in Him and Him in us, then there is a great call on our part to change our mindsets and perspectives of how we see ourselves. When we fail to see the *grace* of God in us, we walk around looking for a miracle without realizing that we are the miracle others are looking for. I'm saying: **"People spend most of their time looking for things they already have!"** Make an inventory of what you have and get busy, don't put your life on hold because of things you don't have.

I find the account of a widow in 2 Kings 4 very interesting. ***"One day the widow of a member of the group of prophets came to Elisha and cried out, "My husband who served you is dead, and you know how he feared the Lord. But now a creditor has come, threatening to take my two sons as slaves."***

"What can I do to help you?" Elisha asked. "Tell me, what do you have in the house?" "Nothing at all, except a flask of olive oil," she replied.

And Elisha said, "Borrow as many empty jars as you can from your friends and neighbors. Then go into your house with your sons and shut the door behind you. Pour olive oil from your flask into the jars, setting each one aside when it is filled."

So she did as she was told. Her sons kept bringing jars to her, and she filled one after another. Soon every container was full to the brim! "Bring me another jar," she said to one of her sons. "There aren't any more!" he told her. And then the olive oil stopped flowing.

When she told the man of God what had happened, he said to her, "Now sell the olive oil and pay your debts, and you and your sons can live on what is left over." 2 Kings 4:1-7 NLT.

It's not hard to imagine just how distraught this woman was. She just lost her husband and now she was about to lose her children. This incident also serves as a prime example of what happens when we fail to apply the principles we have been discussing in this book. Dying and leaving your family with debts, sons about to be sold off into slavery to repay debts is not what God intended. This goes against everything the scriptures teach God's people, yet this type of thing is all around us.

To her credit, this woman didn't just sit around to let fate take its course. She went to look for help. Her situation felt so hopeless, like most people she couldn't see a way out. The woman was looking out there for help like we all do. But the prophet wanted to redirect her focus. Instead of looking outside of herself, he wanted her to take a look deep within herself. **The widow needed a paradigm shift from stressing about what she didn't have to rejoicing in what she had.**

Many times, I find that answers and solutions to most of our pressing needs are not out there! There are right *within* us.

Here is Elisha's response to the woman's cry for help. **"Tell me what do you have in your house?"** What do you have in your house? If you are this woman this question will sound very stupid. The reason she came to seek help from the man of God is because she believed that she had nothing in her house of value. If she thought she had valuables to cover the debt she wouldn't be seeing the prophet.

This reminds me of 1 Corinthians 10:13-14 TPT, ***"We all experience times of testing, which is normal for every human being. But God will be faithful to you. He will screen and filter the severity, nature, and timing of every test or trial you face so that you can bear it. And each test is an opportunity to trust him more, for along with every trial God has provided for you a way of escape that will bring you out of it victoriously."***

Whatever situation we find ourselves in, God has already made a way. For every challenge God allows it packaged with a solution. One of the many names of God is El-Shaddai.

This means to be all-sufficient and self-existent. In a simple way, God has everything He needs at any time for anything already inside Himself. By virtue of being created in His image and likeness, you too have everything you need inside of you to deal with any situation you ever find yourself in. We need to refocus our minds to look deep within ourselves instead of always looking outside for the solution. We can look to people for answers or people can look to us. Remember it's the person with the answers that succeeds and becomes prosperous.

The moment you begin to look inside yourself, you begin to connect with God's destiny within you. Most often than not, it's this connection which unlocks provisions in your life. We all have our favorite movies, music and books. We are willing to part with our hard earned cash just to add these favorites to our collection. But one thing all these movies, music and books have in common is that they began as a little thought or idea inside someone. Someone paid great attention to their little thought and it became the blockbuster we all love which made them rich and wealthy!

Moses once asked God for proof. To his amazement God redirected his focus to what was already in his own hand. ***"But Moses protested again, "What if they won't believe me or listen to me? What if they say, 'The Lord never appeared to you'?" Then the Lord asked him, "What is that in your hand?" "A shepherd's staff," Moses replied. "Throw it down on the ground," the Lord told him. So Moses threw down the staff, and it turned into a snake! Moses jumped back.***

Then the Lord told him, "Reach out and grab its tail." So Moses reached out and grabbed it, and it turned back into a shepherd's staff in his hand. "Perform this sign," the Lord told him. "Then they will believe that the Lord, the God of their ancestors –the God of Abraham, the God of Isaac, and the God of Jacob–really has appeared to you." Exodus 4:1-5 NLT.

May I ask you the same question God asked Moses? What is that in your hand? What do you have? As Moses laid down what was in his hand, it became the proof he was looking for and the very tool God used to free a nation.

When the widow brought the little oil she had to Elisha, she became an instant oil tycoon. I can go on and tell you about the widow who used up her last cup of flour and little oil to make a cake for Elijah. What she thought was her last meal lasted until the famine was over. *Learn to value what you have, it may just be the solution to your need and pathway to your breakthrough!*

"Then the Lord said to Elijah, "Go and live in the village of Zarephath, near the city of Sidon. I have instructed a widow there to feed you."

So he went to Zarephath. As he arrived at the gates of the village, he saw a widow gathering sticks, and he asked her, "Would you please bring me a little water in a cup?" As she was going to get it, he called to her, "Bring me a bite of bread, too."

But she said, "I swear by the Lord your God that I don't have a single piece of bread in the house. And I have only a handful of flour left in the jar and a little cooking oil in the bottom of the jug. I was just gathering a few sticks to cook this last meal, and then my son and I will die."

But Elijah said to her, "Don't be afraid! Go ahead and do just what you've said, but make a little bread for me first.

Then use what's left to prepare a meal for yourself and your son. For this is what the Lord, the God of Israel, says: There will always be flour and olive oil left in your containers until the time when the Lord sends rain and the crops grow again!"

So she did as Elijah said, and she and Elijah and her family continued to eat for many days. There was always enough flour and olive oil left in the containers, just as the Lord had promised through Elijah." 1 Kings 17:8-16 NLT

God always works with what we have. When we focus on what we don't have we miss great opportunities. **Miracles are often found in our response to the usual.** "Sometimes all we have is all we need!"

I can think of a story in John 6:5-13 NLT: ***"Jesus soon saw a huge crowd of people coming to look for him. Turning to Philip, he asked, "Where can we buy bread to feed all these people?"***

He was testing Philip, for he already knew what he was going to do. Philip replied, "Even if we worked for months, we wouldn't have enough money to feed them!" Then Andrew, Simon Peter's brother, spoke up.

"There's a young boy here with five barley loaves and two fish. But what good is that with this huge crowd?" "Tell everyone to sit down," Jesus said. So they all sat down on the grassy slopes. (The men alone numbered about 5,000.) Then Jesus took the loaves, gave thanks to God, and distributed them to the people.

Afterward he did the same with the fish. And they all ate as much as they wanted. After everyone was full, Jesus told his disciples, "Now gather the leftovers, so that nothing is wasted." So they picked up the pieces and filled twelve baskets with scraps left by the people who had eaten from the five barley loaves."

STEWARDSHIP

What do you have is a question of stewardship? This is about making the most of what has been entrusted to us. Use what you have and do what you do and do it well and you will prosper. Don't neglect your talents, develop your skills and maximize your potential and resources.

Paul wrote to young Timothy, ***"Do not neglect the spiritual gift you received through the prophecy spoken over you when the elders of the church laid their hands on you."*** 1 Timothy 4:14 NLT. This principle applies to everything you have, neglect is your worst enemy to success and prosperity. Stewardship opens doors for favor which empowers you to come into your destiny.

In verse 12 of the same chapter Paul gives Timothy another piece of advice, ***"And don't be intimidated by those who are older than you; simply be the example they need to see by being faithful and true in all that you do. Speak the truth and live a life of purity and authentic love as you remain strong in your faith."*** TPT

Believe in who you are don't be intimidated by people, situations and circumstances.

"So, what does all this mean? If God has determined to stand with us, tell me, who then could ever stand against us? For God has proved his love by giving us his greatest treasure, the gift of his Son.

And since God freely offered him up as the sacrifice for us all, he certainly won't withhold from us anything else he has to give." Romans 8:31-32 TPT

GUNG-HO ECONOMICS

Sometimes gung-ho economics is the only way forward. All in or all out! Go big or go home. Making a change in order to break the cycle can be painful. It requires great sacrifice. People don't like change unless it's forced upon them. But it is much easier when we choose to change than being forced to change.

Change is usually initiated by people who are mad enough with the status quo and circumstances.

Mad enough to risk everything just to see a change. Many times, in life it's crazy people who leave a lasting impression and make the difference. It's easy to be nice calm and collected when everything is ok.

NEVER QUIT

For some of us quitting is a luxury we cannot afford! Quitting is only an option if you have other choices. But if it's a choice between this and only this, you must find a way to make it work.

Most people quit because they think quitting is an option. Quitting has a way of creating a gulf between you and your future. When we quit, we are surrendering ourselves at the mercy of our predicament. Predicaments are not gentlemen at all, they will keep on kicking even when you are down. Remember that the battles we fail to win, our kids will have to fight them.

Don't be afraid to reinvent the wheel, sometimes square wheels work better. Like they say, there is method in madness!

CHANGE ONLY HAPPENS WHEN WE DO THINGS DIFFERENTLY.

YOU DON'T STAND OUT BY DOING THE SAME THING AS EVERYONE ELSE.

OTHER BOOKS BY

VC ISAACS

Our identity is embedded in a father. Knowing our heavenly Father unlocks our destiny and launches us into the fullness of what we were created for. To truly know who we are, we need to explore the heart of our Author and Perfecter of our faith whose image and likeness we reflect. Our honor and net-worth is in our Father. The journey from shame to honor is a transaction between my brokenness and the glory of God at work in us. Day-by-day honor shines brighter than shame as we grow from glory to glory.

OTHER BOOKS BY

VC ISAACS

SHAME *to* HONOR

ADOPTED by ABBA

UNLOCKING INTIMACY

TRIUMPH

POWER MEDITATION

Publishing
THR3E 3RED

Made in the USA
Monee, IL
05 November 2026

67808353R00188